The Teaching of Contempt

Jules Isaac

The Teaching of

Translated by Helen Weaver
Biographical Introduction by
Claire Huchet Bishop

Contempt

Christian Roots
of Anti-Semitism

Holt, Rinehart and Winston

New York   Chicago   San Francisco

ACKNOWLEDGMENTS

Grateful acknowledgment is made to the following publishers who have so generously granted permission to reprint from their publications:

Basil Blackwell, Oxford, England, for excerpts from *The Essene Writings from Qumran,* by André Dupont-Sommer, copyright © 1961.

Clarendon Press, Oxford, England, for a passage from *The Apocrypha and Pseudepigrapha of the Old Testament,* edited by R. H. Charles, copyright 1913.

Harper & Row, Publishers, Incorporated, for a passage from *Black Boy,* by Richard Wright, copyright 1945.

Harvard University Press, Cambridge, Massachusetts, and William Heinemann Ltd., London, for excerpts from *Jewish Antiquities,* by Flavius Josephus, translated by Ralph Marcus, from The Loeb Classical Library. Copyright 1943.

Helicon Press, Baltimore, Maryland, for passages from *The Dead Sea Scrolls and Primitive Christianity,* by Jean Daniélou, copyright © 1958 by Helicon Press.

Sheed & Ward Limited, London, for an excerpt from *The Son of God,* by Karl Adam, copyright 1935.

*To the men and women
who have supported and sustained me
in my persistent efforts.*

CONTENTS

THREE MAIN THEMES
OF THE TEACHING OF CONTEMPT

The Teaching of Contempt

JULES ISAAC:

A BIOGRAPHICAL INTRODUCTION

The search for a new relationship between Christians and Jews occupies a special place among the significant developments of our time. The second half of the twentieth century will be known to future generations for spectacular technical achievements, the exploration of space, the emergence of many new nations—all factors emphasizing the essential interdependence of mankind and the desperate seriousness of our search for world unity. But will not historians also be able to see the related character of such phenomena as the ecumenical movement, the more profound appreciation of religious freedom, and—growing out of this spiritual renewal—a serious effort on the part of Christians to re-evaluate Christian teaching regarding the Jews?

We are witnessing something that has been all but unknown in the almost two thousand years of

Christianity. Christians and Jews are beginning
to talk to each other—not simply on public plat-
forms in the cause of patriotism, or to discuss
relatively safe subjects such as social work and
community service, but also about those things that
matter most. What would have been unthinkable
in this country only a few years ago is now being
accepted: Qualified representatives of the two
faiths openly discuss their attitudes toward one
another; there is a face-to-face encounter in which
those who suffered the most on one side, and those
who bear the most responsibility for that suffering on the other, meet in mutual respect.

Of course, there have been Christian voices in
favor of the Jewish people during past centuries.
But these were acts of love on the part of individual
Christians, both popes and humble laymen. Today there appears to be a happy convergence, in
which the most significant spiritual movements
within both Catholic and Protestant Christianity
all point to "a return to the sources," and it is
now easier for Christians to see what was so long
obscured—that our Christian roots are Jewish.

No doubt there are special developments in our
generation that have helped prepare for this newer
and more positive attitude. The creation of the
State of Israel may of itself have reversed many
questionable stereotypes. It would be foolish to
ignore, too, the influence of the powerful and of-

ficially atheistic ideology of communism in leading many in the West to a discovery of their
solidarity with the people to whom Christians owe
the Book. These pragmatic considerations, however real, are only auxiliary. It must be shame-
fully confessed that it took nothing less than the
destruction of European Jewry to awaken the collective Christian conscience. How could Hitler's
Germany have been possible, a country which had
been Christian for fifteen hundred years? The
terrifying responsibility for this unbelievable
cruelty has been underlined by the Protestant
scholar Dr. Bernhard E. Olson: "Hitler's pogrom
was but the crown and pinnacle of a long history of
hatred toward the Jew, participated in (if not
initiated) by those whose duty it was to teach
their children the truths of Christianity!"

For the task of helping Christians accept the im-
plications of this statement, no one could be better
fitted than Jules Isaac. He had the academic
knowledge, the discipline of a scholar, the courage
to speak out, and the nobility to offer the healing
hand of a friendship which is intent on building
for the future. He recognized the degree to which
the martyrdom of his Jewish brothers revealed
an abyss he himself had never suspected. "In
1940," he said shortly before his death, "I thought
first of the defeat of democracy." It was only after
the circle of persecution had widened that "the

Jewish question began to weigh on my mind,
and Jewish solidarity upon my heart and conscience.''

With the hindsight of history, it is hard to understand this delay. Although Hitler's attack on
the Jews had been going on for seven years, apparently even so acute a Frenchman as Jules Isaac
could still believe that it could not happen in his own
country. At the turn of the century, Isaac had
fought for Dreyfus at the side of Charles Péguy;
but once Dreyfus was rehabilitated, Isaac looked
on the *affaire* as an epidemic from which everyone
had recovered.

Professor Isaac did not personally experience
anti-Semitism in the first sixty years of his life. He
was born in 1877, in Rennes, of French-Jewish
parents from Alsace-Lorraine. His grandfather
fought in Napoleon's *Grande Armée,* and his father was a professional army officer. His child-
hood was the conventional one of the son of any
officer stationed in a French provincial town. In
his family, what counted most was devotion to
France and the Republic, and an impeccable sense
of honor.

He pursued an academic career, becoming a professor of history, a humanist, and a widely respected scholar. Every French student knows of
Isaac as the author of the seven-volume *Cours
d'histoire,* long a cornerstone of French and
world history in French secondary schools and

universities. In 1936 Professor Isaac was called
by the French government to the highest office in
his profession, that of Inspector General of Education for the entire country. Throughout these
years, he does not recall any personal anti-Semitic
experiences: "I was a Jew. I did not boast about it
and I did not hide it; it was a fact."

Until 1940 Isaac was known chiefly for his academic achievements and his intellectual integrity.
In addition to the *Cours d'histoire,* he also did
research on the origins of World War I, in which
he had been wounded at Verdun and decorated for
bravery. His book, *Un débat historique: les problèmes des origines de la guerre,* published in 1933,
was later destroyed by the Nazis. He had also
been preoccupied with the suicidal trend of scientific advance, and his essay, "Paradoxe sur la science homicide" (in *Revue de Paris,* 1923), reads
today with the accuracy of prophesy. Twenty-two
years before Hiroshima, Isaac wrote, "In less time
than it takes a volcano to erupt [military tech-
nology] will annihilate cities under a kind of fiery
cloud."

When the Germans occupied France, discrimina-
tory measures were taken, and Professor Isaac
was deprived of his post by the Vichy government. Under the pseudonym of Junius he wrote
Les Oligarques, the story of Athens falling prey
to totalitarian Sparta in the fifth century B.C. It
was a disguised protest and a declaration of dem-

ocratic faith; the analogy with France in 1940 was clear. As Isaac says, "It was a hymn to lost liberty."

As time went on, however, it was the fate of persecuted Israel that became paramount in his thinking. He was of it; it was "a fact." He began to study the phenomenon of anti-Semitism in a deeper perspective, and to ponder its hidden causes. It appeared to him that although the Nazi persecutions were not religious in character, as were those carried on in Christendom in past centuries, there was an historic complicity which could not be explained away. Why was there such silence and apathy in the Christian world concerning the fate of the European Jews? How could Christians sleep during such a night of terror? In 1942 Isaac wrote ten pages on this subject and submitted them to Maurice Blondel and André Trocmé.

In 1943, as he continued working on the problem, tragedy struck. While he was away from their temporary home, at Riom, his wife was arrested by the Gestapo. His daughter, his younger son, his son-in-law, and several other members of his family were seized in Vichy. (His elder son had already fled and was in England.) Except for his younger son, who escaped, all the others were killed by the Nazis. Before Madame Isaac (who had been deeply involved in her husband's work on the Christian roots of anti-Semitism) was shipped to the death camp, she managed to send a clandestine note to her husband. It read, "Save yourself for your work; the world is waiting for it." From then on, this final message from his wife governed Jules Isaac's life.

Fleeing from his persecutors, hiding in farms and many times at the homes of priests or ministers, Professor Isaac took with him his unfinished manuscript and kept working at it, no longer with the detached interest of the historian or the concern of the humanist, but with the passion of his anguished heart. "I viewed my work as a fight for wounded Israel, for brotherhood against hatred. I had a task to fulfill. It was a sacred mission." In 1947 he gave his publisher the six-hundred-page manuscript of *Jésus et Israël*.

The impact of this book in France was considerable—on laymen as well as on the clergy of all faiths. In *Jésus et Israël,* Isaac compares the texts of the Gospels with qualified Catholic and Protestant commentaries. He shows how these commentaries have been so slanted as to give a totally erroneous and distorted picture of Jesus' attitude toward Israel, and of Israel's attitude toward Jesus, as seen in the Gospels. He demonstrates how these inaccurate commentaries—found in books, footnotes, sermons, or catechism lessons—are largely responsible for the Christian's anti-Semitic conditioning. *Jésus et Israël* is no condemnation of authentic Christianity, only of its

shameful and powerful caricature, which helped
to bring unprecedented tragedy on the Jewish
people.

That same year, 1947, Professor Isaac met in
Paris with a group of distinguished Jewish and
Christian intellectuals, including Father Jean de
Menasce, Father Paul Démann, Father Jean
Daniélou, Rev. M. A. Freudenberg, Rabbi Jacob
Kaplan, Rabbi Zwi Taubes, Edmond Fleg, Pro-
fessor F. Lovsky, Jacques Madaule, and Henri
Marrou. He submitted to this group his Eighteen
Points, a specific program for the purification of
Christian teaching regarding the Jews. These were
to form the basis for the Ten Points of Seelisberg,
elaborated later that same year in Switzerland.

From the inception of his work in the field of
Christian-Jewish co-operation, Jules Isaac was
given active encouragement and support by B'nai
B'rith, the international service organization.

In 1948 Professor Isaac created L'Amitié
Judéo-Chrétienne, a French interfaith group
which was to work not only for the complete erad-
ication of false notions in regard to the beliefs of
Jews and Christians, but also for a positive appreciation of each other's heritage.

In 1949, following papal authorization to trans-
late the Good Friday prayer for the Jews, *pro
perfidis judaeis,* using the milder translation "unfaithful" or "unbelieving," Jules Isaac had an
audience with Pope Pius XII. He pointed out to

the Pontiff that the change was insufficient, not only because the wording of the new translation was still objectionable, but also because priests continued to use the Latin word, with its damaging psychological associations. He urged that nothing less than total suppression of the word could be satisfactory. He also mentioned that Catholics did not kneel for the Jews in the Good Friday devotion, and presented the Pope with his Eighteen Points and the Ten Points of Seelisberg. Kneeling for the Jews on Good Friday was re-established in 1955, after nearly twelve centuries. Professor Isaac's work was certainly significant in helping to effect this result.

Isaac published *Genèse de l'antisémitisme* in the following year, 1956. Here he took up the fundamental difference between pagan and Christian anti-Semitism, and argued that the "religious" foundation of the latter made it a more virulent and persistent agent of deep-seated emotional prejudice than its sporadic and rootless pagan counterpart. This work contains further documentation of one of the major themes of the present book, the position of the Jews in the Diaspora prior to the destruction of Jerusalem in A.D. 70.

With one stroke of the pen, Pope John XXIII, in 1958, eliminated the word *perfidis* in the prayer for the Jews, both in Latin and in the vernacular. In 1959 he did away with two other prejudicial sentences, one in the Act of Consecration to the Sacred Heart, recited every First Friday, the other in the ritual of baptism of converts.

Highly encouraged by these actions of the Pope, Professor Isaac praised him in a lecture at the Sorbonne (December 15, 1959), and appealed for direct, unequivocal, and final condemnation of the age-old teaching of contempt for the Jews: "Let it disappear forever from books that are called Christian, and lips that are called Christian." The lecture was published in France the following year, and was translated into English by Professor and Mrs. James Parkes, of Oxford, under the title, "Has Anti-Semitism Roots in Christianity?" An American edition was distributed in 1961 by the National Conference of Christians and Jews, with a foreword by Cardinal Cushing, of Boston, and an introductory essay by Dr. Olson.

There have been a number of other encouraging signs since Professor Isaac began his work, whether directly or indirectly sparked by his contribution. The World Council of Churches, in their meeting at New Delhi in 1961, adopted a resolution that reflected its concern with the subject of this book. Under the direction of Dr. Anker Gjerding, director of its committee on the Church and the Jewish People, it has undertaken a program of considerable promise. In the United States, too, important groundwork has been laid, especially by the Anti-Defamation League of B'nai B'rith and the American Jewish Committee. Prot-

estant and Catholic scholars have engaged in a serious analysis of catechisms, missals, Sunday-school
texts, and other materials used in the religious
education of the young, with the aim of eliminating
offensive and unchristian references to Jews. The
Protestant self-study project, *Faith and Prejudice,*
by Bernhard E. Olson, was published by the Yale
University Press in 1963; the Catholic study, by
Sister M. Rose Albert Thering, *The Self-Concept
Potential in Religion Texts,* was an unpublished
Ph.D. dissertation at St. Louis University in 1961.*
The examples of personal commitment to a work
of reparation and disinterested scholarship de-
serves a more extended tribute.

Nevertheless, practical results, however hope-
ful, remained fragmentary and insufficient, and
Jules Isaac decided he should make one further
effort. There seemed to be a special relevance in
seeking an audience with Pope John XXIII, who
had already given proof of his willingness to denounce abuses, and who had just called the Roman
Catholic Church into Council.

The private audience was granted in 1960, and
the two venerable men sat side by side in a lengthy,
earnest, and friendly conversation. Professor
Isaac made a brief summary of the results of his
research, and presented his request. He pointed

---

* A similar Jewish self-study, directed by Dr. Bernard D. Wein-
ryb, has been conducted at Dropsie College for Hebrew and
Cognate Learning in Philadelphia.

out that although there had been a reversal of attitude on the part of many individual Catholics, both during and after the war, nothing conclusive had yet been done. There was a crying need for the voice of the head of the Church to be heard, solemnly and forever condemning "the teaching of contempt."

Then Professor Isaac presented his own practical suggestion, the creation of a subcommission in the Council, especially empowered to study this question. The Pope, who had been listening attentively and sympathetically, declared spontaneously, "I have been thinking about that ever since you began to speak." A subcommission of the Secretariat for Promoting Christian Unity has now been brought into existence, under the leadership of Cardinal Augustin Bea, and has already made a noticeable impression.* Isaac thanked the Pope for

* At the second session of the current Vatican Council, a statement on the Church's attitude to the Jews, presented as point four in the schema on ecumenism, was distributed to the bishops. (It is expected that it will be voted on at the third session.) This document, asserting that it is wrong and harmful to blame the Jews for Jesus' death, was issued from the Secretariat for the Promotion of Christian Unity, headed by Cardinal Bea, with whom Jules Isaac had a long talk following the papal audience. At the time, Cardinal Bea favored Professor Isaac's idea of the subcommission, and promised him to ask His Holiness that it be made part of the Secretariat for the Promotion of Christian Unity. Thus the declaration of October 17, 1963, bears the mark of the intervention, first and foremost, of Jules Isaac who, unfortunately, did not live to see this memorable result.

earlier actions which had aroused great hopes
among Jews, and added, "Because of his great
kindness, is not the Pope himself responsible if
we now expect more?"

To dramatize this atmosphere of expectancy,
Professor Isaac, at the age of eighty-five, wrote
The Teaching of Contempt, the first of his books
to be published in English. We cannot help wish-
ing that it had been written by a Christian. But
this does not diminish our humble admiration for
this noble scholar, who was a Jew and who, rising
above personal grief and righteous wrath, accepted as his primary obligation the appeal, firm
but without rancor, to the conscience of his Christian brothers.

CLAIRE HUCHET BISHOP

FOREWORD

We are all familiar with the words of Jesus from the Fourth Gospel, "In my Father's house are many mansions" (John 14:2). I fear that in Satan's house there are even more—if only to accommodate the thousand varieties of anti-Semitism whose most virulent form in our day would seem to be Hitler's racial anti-Semitism.

Need I apologize, then, for carrying on my struggle to expose—and, if possible, to extirpate—the Christian roots of anti-Semitism? No, for in my opinion they are the deepest ones of all.

I am told that I would do better to devote myself to some constructive task: rather than denounce the teaching of contempt, why not initiate the teaching of respect?

But the two ends are inseparable. It is impossible to combat the teaching of contempt and its modern survivals, without thereby laying the foundations for the teaching of respect; and, conversely, it is impossible to establish the teaching of

17

respect, without first destroying the remnants of the teaching of contempt. Truth cannot be built upon error.

A work of purification is never a negative activity. For us, such an effort is an essential preliminary, which we shall never cease to recommend to every Christian conscience.

JULES ISAAC

Preliminary
Considerations

"There is something worse than having an evil mind, and that is having a closed one."
—Charles Péguy

"It is a fundamental rule of life never to distort the truth."
—Pope John XXIII

1

All authorities are agreed that a true Christian cannot be an anti-Semite.

Let us begin by recalling that the term *anti-Semitism* is used nowadays to refer to anti-Jewish prejudice, to feelings of suspicion, contempt, hostility, and hatred toward Jews, both those who follow the religion of Israel and those who are merely of Jewish parentage.

Given this, here is my first statement of principle: All authorities are agreed that anti-Semitism is by definition unchristian, even anti-Christian. A true Christian cannot be an anti-Semite; he simply has no right to be one.

"The Church teaches that there is only one human race, and that by nature all men are and always will be brothers, not only by virtue of their common origin, but also for a still more exalted reason, the universal redemption of man, which

Jesus Christ, through the operation of grace, accomplished by his death on the cross." This is why "anti-Semitism amounts to a form of anti-Christianity." (L. T. Devaux, Superior-General of the Missionary Priests of Our Lady of Zion)

"Anti-Semitic hatred is an anti-Christian madness which would render meaningless the martyrdom and death of Jesus." (Jacques Maritain)

"The teachings of the Church compel us, from both the human and the religious points of view, to reject anti-Semitism utterly and to adopt toward the Jewish people an attitude of love and respect which is its antithesis." (Pastoral letter of Cardinal Liénart, Bishop of Lille)

"Anti-Semitism . . . is a movement in which we Christians can have no part. . . . Anti-Semitism is inadmissible. Spiritually we are Semites. . . . Through Christ and in Christ, we are spiritual offspring of Abraham." (Address by Pope Pius XI in 1938 to a group of Belgian pilgrims)

Moreover, as of March 25, 1928, anti-Semitism is officially condemned by a Decree of the Holy Office: "The Apostolic See . . . even as it disapproves of all envy and jealousy among nations, so it condemns in an especial manner the hatred against the people once chosen by God, that hatred, namely, which nowadays is commonly called anti-Semitism."

The Protestants add their voices to those of the Catholics:

"Anti-Semitism is a sin against the Holy Ghost,

because it implies the rejection of divine grace."
(Karl Barth)

"For the Church, anti-Semitism is the most
grievous denial of Christ, the most insidious per-
version of the Gospel of the Incarnation. For the
world, it is the proof of essential idolatry and
fundamental barbarousness." (The Reverend
Charles Westphal)

"We declare anti-Semitism to be a plain denial
of the spirit of our Lord. A Christian cannot be
anti-Semitic in thought, word, or deed without being unfaithful to his Christian heritage." (Statement of the Federal Council of Churches in Amer-
ica, 1938)

"We call upon all the churches we represent to
denounce anti-Semitism, no matter what its origin,
as absolutely irreconcilable with the profession
and practice of the Christian faith. Anti-Semitism
is sin against God and man." (Resolution of the
World Council of Churches, Amsterdam, 1948)

2

*And yet, consciously or subcon-
sciously, anti-Semitism is profoundly
rooted in Christianity.*

My second contention is diametrically opposed
to the preceding one, but it is nevertheless a state-

ment of fact: There is a Christian anti-Semitism.
Whether conscious or subconscious, it is perennial
and virulent, of great scope and intensity. It may
be affirmed with complete confidence that the vast
majority of Christians—or those recognized as
such—are anti-Semites. For even in the best Christians, even in those who fought most courageously
against Nazi anti-Semitism, it is easy to distinguish traces of a kind of subconscious anti-Semitism.

There is no better example of this than the perpetual distortion of Jewish history by Christian
theologians. When I read, in *Pax nostra,* a book
published in 1936 by Father Gaston Fessard, S.J.,
a chapter entitled, "The Negative Mission and
Destiny of the Jewish People," I submit that this
very title, referring to a people to whom the Christians owe the Bible and the concept of monotheism,
is itself a tendentious denial revealing subconscious prejudice. It is exposed throughout the
chapter, as the author points to "the murderous
race . . . eternally riveted at the crossroads
where the destinies of mankind meet and intersect, in order to point out to passers-by the direction of history." He even tries to prove that "having rejected Christ in order to save their native
land, the Jews have been rejected from their land,
and their persistent nonassimilation in the midst
of other races remains the indelible proof of their
providential punishment." Such an interpretation

of God's will is all the more ill-advised in that it rests on a dubious understanding of the historical facts.

There are similar problems in some articles by a well-known Protestant theologian, Professor Franz J. Leenhardt, writing from Geneva in those years between 1938 and 1941 that saw the beginning of the great martyrdom of the European Jews. "Why," he asks, "from the moment they came in contact with the world, have the Jews ultimately been intolerable to it? Why is this race—if race it be—why is this people and this nation intolerable to all, when they possess such outstanding qualities that at times one almost feels that the Jewish miracle is equal to the Greek?" This does not prevent the same author from asserting later that "Israel exhibited none of those human qualities which one would be justified in demanding of a people who claimed to be God's chosen race, and its history furnishes abundant proof that it was unworthy of this name." To me it is clear that such contradictory statements point to a state of mind, and that while ostensibly refuting anti-Semitism, by his very choice of words Professor Leenhardt has adopted its most questionable arguments.

Yes, even after Auschwitz, Maidenek, Dubno, and Treblinka, Christian anti-Semitism is still alive. It does not perceive, it does not wish to perceive the hidden bond linking it with Nazi anti-

Semitism, whose anti-Christian racism has committed such unspeakable ravages. Unwilling to become aware of its own responsibilities despite the efforts of a courageous minority, it continues to be widely disseminated in the classroom, in the catechism, from the pulpit, and in literature. For proof of this I would refer my readers to my earlier book, *Jésus et Israël,* and to Father Paul Démann's study of the way in which official catechisms deal with "The people of the Bible." Up to now the inquiry covers only French-speaking Catholicism.[1]

3

It will be objected that anti-Semitism has always existed; but this argument has no solid historical foundation.

Certain persons, and they are legion, will be quick to counter these preliminary considerations with that argument dear to theologians; namely, the agelessness and universality of anti-Semitism. It is their contention that anti-Semitism existed in all times, in all places, long before the Christian era.

The implication is that Christianity would thus

be in no way responsible—as though it were not
responsible for its own attitude in any event.
Rather, the responsibility would rest with the
Jewish people themselves because of their religious intransigence, their separatism, their "persistent nonassimilation" in the midst of others.

"Not only today, but from the beginning of their
existence, the Jews have been looked upon as an
alien group, a thorn in the flesh of humanity."
(Memorandum of the Theological Committee of
the Swiss Evangelical Society)

"Anti-Semitism is as old as Judaism itself, the
very essence of which is to refuse to accommodate
itself to the mind and manners of other peoples
and to provoke universal antipathy." (Hermann
Gunkel, quoted by W. Vischer, *Esther*)

But are these popular notions supported by history? Absolutely not.

On the historical level there is nothing to justify
the assertion that anti-Semitism was present from
the beginning of Israel's history. That a pagan
anti-Semitism existed in antiquity is incontestable,
but it turns out to have been much more localized
in time and space than is generally believed.

The argument of "universal anti-Semitism" has
no more historical foundation than that of "eternal anti-Semitism." The Jews who were deported
to Chaldea in the sixth century B.C. lived there
quietly and prosperously for several centuries;
Babylonia became one of the principal centers of

Judaism. The Jews who emigrated to China encountered no hostility, and eventually disappeared into the mass of the Chinese population.

All of which proves that the "persistent nonassimilation" of the Jews has no more foundation than the assumption that preceded it. It could even be maintained that Israel has a natural gift for assimilation: throughout history there have always been assimilable and assimilated elements in Jewish culture, depending upon the reception the Jews have encountered, the environment in which they have found themselves. This is easily verified in our own time. How many European Jews have distinguished themselves as writers of national importance, as thinkers, scholars, Nobel prize winners, statesmen?

Religious intransigence must not be confused with cultural nonassimilation. On the religious level, from ancient times Jewish piety has proved unyielding in its exclusive loyalty to the One God and to his Law, the Torah. For the Jews, living scattered among pagan peoples, this loyalty entailed a certain separatism; and all separatism breeds feelings of suspicion, hostility, and scorn due to lack of understanding. This has been the primary source of anti-Semitism, and it is essentially religious.

Have Christians and Moslems the right to reproach the Jews for their separatism? Without it, without their religious intransigence in a pagan

world, the Jews would not have handed on to the
Christians, or to Islam, the torch of monotheism,
the belief in One All-powerful and Eternal God.

"Which commandment is the first of all?" one
of the scribes asks Jesus, and Jesus answers (Mark
12: 28–29): "Hear, O Israel: The Lord our God,
the Lord is one."

4

Pagan, pre-Christian anti-Semitism,
whose center was Alexandria, was of
the most vulgar sort.

Without repeating all the arguments I have often
made elsewhere, above all in *Genèse de l'antisé-*
mitisme, I think I should review their essential
points.

To be sure, anti-Jewish prejudice and the persecution of Jews were known before the Christian
era. Echoes are to be found in the Bible, particularly in the books of Exodus, Esther, and the
Maccabees. Formal history does not establish this
pagan anti-Semitism until rather late—notably
during the two centuries immediately before the
birth of Jesus and the two immediately after. Its
chief center was in Egypt, at the great metropolis

of Alexandria, where there was a bitter rivalry between the Greeks and the Jews. This economic
competition is the second source of anti-Semitism,
at least so far as the Greeks are concerned. As for
the Romans, their principal grievance against the
Jews was that they were a seditious, ungovern-
able people; three major rebellions, which Roman
power had so much trouble putting down, inflamed
that Roman pride which Tacitus elects to interpret
for us: *Augebat iras quod soli Judaei non ces-
sissent* ("[Roman] tempers flared because only the
Jews refused to yield").

On close examination, what strikes one is the
tasteless vulgarity of this pagan anti-Semitism.
With what does it charge the Jews? With hatred
of humanity; with contempt for the pagan gods,
compounded with the most absurd superstitions;
with such loathsome and ridiculous religious practices as adoring a golden ass's head; with the
ritual murder of a Greek fattened for the occasion.
(The pagans found no better charges to make
against the first Christians—except that the ritual
murder attributed to the Christians took the form
of infanticide.) [2] The Latin authors condemn the
Jewish Sabbath as a reprehensible sign of laziness,
because the Jewish custom of weekly rest spread
rapidly throughout the Roman world.

In his treatise *On Superstition*, Seneca condemned "the sacred things of the Jews, and especially the Sabbaths, declaring that "they act use-

lessly in keeping every seventh day, whereby they
lose through idleness about the seventh part of
their life," but he admits that this Jewish custom
has been "received in all lands." (Text cited in
Saint Augustine, *City of God,* vi, 10)

At any rate, it is an error to state that the Jews
have always been subjected to intolerance, and
persecuted by the pagans. The reverse is true: the
persecutions were spasmodic, and more often than
not the Jews enjoyed the good will of the government. The Ptolemies of Egypt esteemed them and
employed them as soldiers, customs inspectors, col-
onists, and revenue officers; it appears that Jews
served as commanding officers of the Egyptian
army. In the Roman Empire, the religion of the
Jews was the only foreign creed to be *licita,* or
officially tolerated; it had a powerful attraction
for a great many people, and every synagogue
had its sympathizing, or "God-fearing," pagans.
None of this agrees with the "scorn" and "universal antipathy" which so many historians cite
without offering sufficient evidence.

Nor is there any more truth in the assertion that
the Jews exhibited from ancient times "that gift
for making money which earned them such re-
nown." [3] In his authoritative *Verus Israël,* Marcel
Simon observes that at the time of the Roman
Empire, "when one considers the empire as a
whole, the Jewish population included a large
majority of poor people. . . . The complaint most

often made against the Jews is not that they were
rolling in wealth, but that they were ragged and
dirty.''

5

*Christian anti-Semitism, which is
essentially theological, has been
infinitely more pernicious and
persistent, since it has continued up to our own time.*

Everyone knows, or at least should know, that
it was from Judaism that Christianity was born.
It was at first simply a Jewish sect, which tried
at the beginning to rally the Jewish people
through the preaching of its Jewish apostles. In
this it was not without success, for in spite of
the opposition of the authorities, according to
the Acts of the Apostles, a growing number of
adherents were received into the new faith.

However, after the last third of the first century, primitive Judeo-Christianity gave way to a
violent Judeo-Christian antagonism. The reasons
for this are mysterious and complex.[4] We shall
confine ourselves here to the essential fact: from
the moment that Christianity, turning toward the

"gentiles"—the pagan peoples—broke with the Law of Moses, the Torah, it was bound to encounter hostility from a Judaism still faithful to that Law.

From this essential fact derives another of vital importance. For the Christian apostolate in pagan lands, there was nothing more irritating or more galling than the passionate resistance of the Jews which they encountered everywhere, their refusal to recognize Jesus as Christ (or Messiah) and as Son of God in the fullest sense of the word—that is, as his "only Son." In the eyes of the pagan world this obstinate refusal was a stunning contradiction of Christian teachings. To overcome this obstacle was all the more a vital necessity, in that for a long time the Synagogue continued to exert a powerful attraction not only over the pagans, but also over a large group of Christian converts still prone to "Judaizing."

How could the Christians succeed? Only by destroying the prestige of their adversary, by a campaign to discredit him. Indeed, this was a constant aim of Christian apologetics, and was already noticeable in many passages of the four canonical Gospels. It became even more obvious in the apocryphal Gospels, and reached its height with the Church Fathers of the fourth century. From then on, the victorious Church was allied with the Empire, and caution was no longer necessary.

Objective history bears all this out, and sees in

it the source of Christian anti-Semitism. The impartial Marcel Simon writes: "Unlike pagan anti-Semitism, which is more apt to consist of a spontaneous reaction, [Christian anti-Semitism] is exceptionally well directed and organized toward a precise end: to render the Jews hateful." [5] It has, moreover, "an official, systematic and unified quality which has always been lacking in the former. It is at the service of theology and is fed by her; it borrows her arguments . . . in a special kind of exegesis of biblical interpretation . . . for what amounts to a long indictment of the chosen people."

In this manner was established a kind of so-called Christian teaching which is more accurately called the Teaching of Contempt, and which I have shown to be the most formidable and pernicious weapon ever used against Judaism or the Jews. But contempt for Judaism is nothing less than contempt for the truth. In order to complete this proof it appears necessary to examine here some of the typical arguments of the teaching of contempt—theological myths which overreach everywhere the bounds of historical and even of scriptural accuracy.

It must be clearly understood that to oppose the teaching of contempt is not to oppose a doctrine essential to the Christian faith. On the contrary, the object of our attack is a tradition, time-honored and therefore all the more powerful, influential, and destructive, but in no way normative from the religious point of view. It is a tradition with confused origins, ill-defined aims, and diverse interpretations; it is, in fact, more a custom than a tradition, a custom made up of deep-seated prejudices and of the most odious habits of mind, heart, and tongue.

These habits, so ominous because of the feelings they produce in defenseless minds, and the hateful, sometimes criminal deeds which are their inevitable consequence—is it not time we broke their spell? To this work I challenge all Christian hearts, all those who passionately desire the day when Love shall triumph over Hate. And I challenge, too, the highest authorities of the Christian Church, repeating with all the force of a burning conviction what I said in a lecture at the Sorbonne on December 15, 1959: "The teaching of contempt has been with us long enough. It has wrought enough evil in the world. It no longer has the right to exist. God grant that it may be solemnly condemned, not only condemned but banished, abolished and utterly obliterated, that it may disappear forever from all books and all lips which call themselves Christian."

NOTES

1 Jules Isaac, *Jésus et Israël* (Paris, 1948; reissued 1959). Paul Démann, *La catéchèse chrétienne et le peuple de la*

Bible (Paris, 1952). Father Démann has announced a second investigation covering new editions and new French catechetic publications between 1951 and 1961; its results will enable us to see what progress has been made.

2 See Jules Isaac, "Histoire ancienne de la fable du crime rituel," *Evidences,* October, 1950.

3 See Pierre Jouguet, *La vie municipale dans l'Egypte romaine* (Paris, 1911).

4 See Jules Isaac, *Genèse de l'antisémitisme* (Paris, 1956), pp. 143–154. A shorter treatment of the same subject has been translated and issued in pamphlet form by the National Conference of Christians and Jews under the title *Has Anti-Semitism Roots in Christianity?* (1961)

5 Marcel Simon, *Verus Israël* (Paris, 1948), p. 263.

Three Main Themes of the Teaching of Contempt

I
THE DISPERSION OF THE JEWS AS A PROVIDENTIAL PUNISHMENT

II
THE DEGENERATE STATE OF JUDAISM AT THE TIME OF JESUS

III
THE CRIME OF DEICIDE

Man's ability to perceive the truth represents a solemn and sacred responsibility to co-operate in the design of his Creator, Redeemer, and Glorifier. . . .

How splendid, in this light, is that invitation extended to him always to speak the truth to his neighbor, and how mighty and dreadful that commandment never to bear false witness against him. . . .

The truth sets us free. It ennobles the man who pronounces it openly and without regard for the opinion of men. . . . The man who has the truth is assured of having with him the light that dispels all darkness and the irresistible power that can transform the world. . . .

As we contemplate an ideal which consists in honoring, thinking, saying and doing the truth, and the daily spectacle of the betrayal of this idea, whether in public or private, Our heart cannot master its grief, and Our voice trembles. . . .

—POPE JOHN XXIII
Christmas Message, 1960

I

THE DISPERSION OF THE JEWS:
PROVIDENTIAL PUNISHMENT
FOR THE CRUCIFIXION

1

*We must make a distinction between
the Dispersion as historical fact and
as theological myth.*

The Dispersion of the Hebrew people, usually referred to by its Greek name, *Diaspora,* is a problem of great importance on the historical as well
as the theological plane.

But the endless commentaries which have been
written on this subject for almost two thousand
years, and above all the theological commentaries,
have sown confusion in men's minds, as well as

hatred in their hearts; they have obscured the
most obvious truths, contradicted the evidence,
and entirely distorted the perspectives of history.

Hence our first proposition, that it is necessary
to make a distinction between the Dispersion as
historical fact and the Dispersion as theological
myth.

This formula may strike some readers as odd
and even irreverent. Let me assure you in all sin-
cerity that I mean no irreverence toward theology,
and still less toward the Christian religion. As an
historian, and one little given to theological specu-
lation, I am well aware that theology by its very
nature goes beyond history in a unique way. But it
is also true that in all the great religions, theology
has an intimate connection with history. So it is
with those three religions which may be said to be
members of the same family—the Jewish, the
Christian, and the Moslem—since the divine revelation, the mystery of faith which is fundamental
to these three religions, becomes part of their history. For the Jewish believer, this takes place
through God's covenant with Abraham and the
choosing of the Hebrew people; for the Christian,
through the coming of Jesus Christ and the mystery of the Incarnation; and for the Moslem,
through the life and mission of Mohammed. Therefore, history has a right to hold theology account-
able for the use the latter has made of the historical data at her disposal. History has a right to ask

theology not to distort or misconstrue these data
and to remain conscientiously faithful to historical
truth, insofar as the latter can be fairly ascer-
tained and determined. It is true that theology
goes beyond history, but only provided that theology respect history as its point of departure; this
is not only its duty but, I venture to say, its sacred
duty, for as I have said in discussing a passage
from the great Protestant theologian Karl Barth,[1]
"the truth belongs to God."

However, regarding the Dispersion of Israel—
one is tempted to say, regarding almost the whole
history of the Hebrew people, and especially their
post-biblical history—Christian theology has disseminated ideas which not only depart from historical truth, but which often distort and contradict it in such a way that they may justly be termed
myths—ideas of a character and content more appropriate to legend than to history.

The good faith of those responsible is not in
question; they have not acted consciously or sys-
tematically. These myths have their origin in passionate controversies which took place, during the
first centuries of the Christian era, between the
scholars of the old Law and those of the new
Church, the men referred to as the Church Fathers.[2] For one reason or another, polemics always constitute an unreliable source, an unfortunate point of departure.

And, in fact, Christian theology, once started in
this direction, never stopped. Utterly convinced of
its rights, it has repeated and propagated these
mythical arguments tirelessly, with methodical
thoroughness, through all the powerful means that
were—and still are—at its disposal, for hundreds
upon hundreds of years, its thousands and thousands of voices indoctrinating each successive generation. How can we overlook this essential fact if
we wish to understand certain aspects of the Jewish question, even today?

The result is that the myths propagated in this
manner have eventually taken on the shape and
consistency of facts, of facts that have become
incontestable. They have ended up by being accepted as though they were authentic history. They
have become an integral part of Christian thinking; nay, of the thinking of all educated people
living in a traditionally Christian civilization.
For what is most surprising is that neither free
thinkers nor the Jews themselves have hesitated
to accept these myths. What is more, they have
even helped to disseminate them—so complete has
been the victory of theology or the defeat of history.

This is what I should like to try to demonstrate
briefly, by examining first the myth of the Dispersion as it has been and still is generally taught,
and then the historical fact of the Dispersion as it

appears in its complex reality to anyone who studies it with an open mind.

2

Christian theology commonly teaches that the Dispersion of Israel, dated at A.D. *70, is the divine punishment for the Crucifixion.*

Theology commonly teaches that the Dispersion of Israel is a divine, a providential punishment. On this subject, history is silent; it has nothing to say, absolutely nothing to add; it is beyond its depth. At most, it can make this simple statement: that it is the rule for all religions, all theologies, to present a people's old or new misfortunes as punishment for their sins, a punishment in accordance with the will of God. One has only to open the Hebrew Bible to find many examples. This is one point on which the Jewish and Christian theologies—otherwise so much opposed—are in agreement.

But here is the delicate point at which their differences confront each other: Christian theology teaches that the Dispersion of Israel is the

divine punishment for the Crucifixion. Now, according to the deductions of qualified experts, it
seems probable that the crucifixion of Jesus must
be placed chronologically around A.D. 29 or 30.
Thus it is absolutely necessary that the Dispersion of Israel, or at least the final dispersion, be
somewhat later than 29 or 30. What Christian
theology commonly teaches is that it occurred forty
years after the Crucifixion, in the year 70. And indeed, 70 was a disastrous year for Israel, since it
was the year of the capture of Jerusalem by Titus,
son of the Emperor Vespasian, after four years
spent in one of the cruelest and bloodiest wars
ever waged by the great and powerful Roman Empire, with all its armed might—against whom?
Against a small rebellious nation, the Jews of
Palestine. The year 70 is not only the date of the
capture of Jerusalem by Titus, but of the destruction of the Second Temple, the one sanctuary of
Hebrew orthodoxy.

That the fatal year 70 marks the end of the
Jewish nation and the beginning of its dispersion
throughout the world is a very popular assertion
of Christian theology from the most ancient times,
at least from the third century, as we find in the
eloquent prose of Tertullian and Origen. The latter writes, "It accordingly [because they committed a crime of the most unhallowed kind] be-
hoved that city where Jesus underwent these suf-
ferings to perish utterly, and the Jewish nation

to be overthrown. . . ."[3] Almost all the Church
Fathers of the fourth century speak with the same
voice, from Saint Ephrem to Saint Jerome, from
Saint John Chrysostom to Saint Augustine. In
the great Augustinian treatise *The City of God*
we read: "But the Jews who rejected him, and
slew him, . . . after that were miserably spoiled
by the Romans . . . and dispersed over the face
of the whole earth."[4] Before such a pronounce-
ment, from such distinguished pens, how could the
Church hesitate? She believed it with all her heart,
and upheld it with all her authority. The illustrious
Pope Gregory the Great (590–604), whose writings
formed the cornerstone of Christian instruction in
the Middle Ages, is no less categorical than Saint
Augustine or Origen: "The apostles had scarcely
set foot on the land of exile when Judea fell to
Titus; her people, driven forth, were scattered all
over the earth."[5]

From then on, century after century, the theme
is taken up in varying tones—above all, alas, the
tone of contempt. Glancing through a seventh-
century apologetic text of the Eastern Church, I
came upon the following passage: "Covered with
disgrace and rejected by all nations from the moment Christ was crucified, [the Jews] have been
scattered far and wide, they have become the servants of all the peoples of the earth, because they
did not believe in Christ."[6] It would be easy but
tiresome to demonstrate that almost all Christian

writers have elaborated this theme since those distant days when, it must be recognized, the search for historical accuracy was the least of their concerns.

To skip across the centuries to our own time: Although there have been some scholarly studies on the Dispersion of Israel,[7] some excellent syntheses of the history of Israel, nevertheless the tradition remains fixed: nothing, it would seem, can shatter it now. The same theme continues to reappear, expressed as categorically and confidently as ever by authors whom we would expect to be better informed.

Take, for example, Father F. M. Braun, O.P.: "When the Jewish people were punished and scattered in the disaster of 70 . . ."[8] Or Father Fessard, S.J.: "Jesus had foretold it: the Jewish people was to be scattered. A few dozen years after the death of Jesus . . . scattered to the four winds of the earth. . . . The Christian tradition has made no mistake about this. It regards . . . the dispersion of Israel as a divine punishment: having rejected Christ in order to save their country, the Jews have been rejected from their land, and their persistent nonassimilation in the midst of other races remains the indelible proof of their providential punishment."[9] Or Father Ferdinand Prat, S.J., whose widely translated two-volume work, *Jesus Christ,* has been recommended reading for priests and seminarians in many countries: "The vengeance of God will descend without mercy on this deicide people. . . . The miserable remnants of Israel will be scattered throughout the vastness of the world, where they must bear until the end of time the weight of this mysterious malediction." [10] Indeed, certain Catholic authors have gone so far as to present this Jewish dispersion in 70 as "conclusive proof of the divinity of Christianity as against the Jews." [11]

And one could add a great many Protestant authors to their number.

Thus Professor Franz Leenhardt: "The people which was to find its fulfillment in the coming of the awaited Messiah, denied that Messiah; and behold them, henceforth broken, scattered, rejected by men, and in the eyes of faith, rejected by God." [12]

Thus the Reverend Jean Bosc: "The Jews refused to acknowledge their king; they mocked him, condemned him to death, crucified him. . . . They denied God to His face. . . . And God [punished] them. He took away the land he had given them as the sign of his promise. . . . They are scattered over the surface of the earth, without a land of their own [written in 1946] . . . with a religion robbed of its substance." [13]

And thus, at the top of the list, Karl Barth himself: "According to all the rules of world history [the Jews] should have disappeared from the in-

ternational scene after the fall of Jerusalem in the
year 70 of our era [by implication: because of the
Diaspora]. Why were they not swallowed up in
the sea of other peoples? . . . There is good reason
to wonder very seriously whether, after the year 70,
one still has a right to talk about a common history
of the Jews." [14]

And these are writings of authors of some talent
and reputation—you may imagine the rest. . . .

3

*The assertion has been made so cate-
gorically and repeated for so many
centuries that it has passed into
standard works of history.*

When century after century a theological argument is repeated in this way, when it is presented
by respected and respectable authors with such
absolute conviction, it comes to be accepted without any verification as a commonplace. It leaves
theology behind and becomes a part of history.

Let us turn first to the books used in religious
schools to teach Catholic children sacred history,
or even secular history. Here we meet again the
familiar assertion that the Dispersion of the Jew-

ish people was a punishment for the Crucifixion, and dated from the year 70; and more often than not, we also find in these books the familiar tone of contempt toward the Jews.

An example which I first quoted in *Jésus et Israël* is taken from a manual published in 1947, one year before the declaration of independence of the State of Israel: "The punishment of the Jews who had committed the crime of deicide was not long in coming. Thirty-six years after the death of the Saviour, the Roman Emperor Titus seized Jerusalem. . . . The Jews, scattered all over the world, never succeeded in re-establishing a nation. They wandered everywhere, looked on as a race accursed, an object of contempt to other peoples." The immediate result of my quoting this passage was that one of the authors of the manual made a very decent apology for having allowed the circulation of such ideas. Let us hope that they were later corrected. But what if no one had called attention to them?

Since the publication of *Jésus et Israël* and the adoption of the Seelisberg Ten Points by The International Congress of Christians and Jews, certain courageous Catholics have become deeply and wholeheartedly involved in the work that has been outlined. From 1950 to 1952 they undertook a laborious investigation of over two thousand French-language books of Catholic instruction then in use; they published the results of their investigation in a report, *La catéchèse chrétienne et le peuple de la Bible,* with a preface by Cardinal Saliège. Their findings exceeded our gloomiest predictions; they demonstrate the urgent necessity for the reform we have never ceased to advocate.

The investigators reported: ''That Jesus Christ foretold the destruction of Jerusalem and the dispersion of the Jewish people as the punishment for their rejection of their Messiah is the classic argument repeated by almost all the manuals—an argument,'' they have the courage to add, ''prompted neither by the Gospels nor by history.''

Here is one example from among a thousand: ''Jerusalem and the Jewish people were visibly punished by the hand of God. . . . The Temple of Jerusalem was destroyed, and with it the religion of Moses ceased to exist. From that time the Jews wandered homeless, exiled, over the face of the earth.''

Here is another, offered in answer to the question, ''Were Jesus' prophecies fulfilled?'' ''. . . History teaches us that in the year 70 . . . the survivors were scattered, and from then on the 'Jewish race' never succeeded, despite all its repeated efforts, in rebuilding a nation.''

And another: ''From that time [70] the Jews lived scattered all over the world; they should realize only too well that they had sinned in killing the Lord.''

A final example: ''. . . The destruction of Jeru-

salem by the Romans [70] and the final dispersion
of the Jews throughout the empire soon consummated the abrogation of the Law and the punishment of the unbelieving deicide people.'' [15]

We must allow the plea of extenuating circumstances, however, in the case of authors of text-
books (of whom I myself am one). It is not their
responsibility to recapitulate the scholarly work
of historical reconstruction; they have simply
drawn on what they believed to be good sources,
repeating what a great number of established
writers had said before them. And it may be
said that they are in good company, for our theological myth has penetrated everywhere, even into
recent works, including some by Jewish authors,
by professional historians, and by qualified scholars of the highest academic level.

Here are two typical examples:

In a careful study published in 1948, Marcel
Braunschwig, a distinguished Jewish scholar and
teacher, writes: ''In the year 70 the Jews were
driven out of the land of their ancestors and blown
across the world like dust. . . . It would be hard
to exaggerate the historical importance of this
dispersion of the Jews: few events have had so
many unforeseen consequences, whose repercus-
sions are still felt in our time.'' [16]

Or, better still, in Fliche and Martin's great
History of the Church, known and used by all stu-
dents of history, over the signature of the historian

Louis Bréhier, university professor and member of the French Institute, we read: "After the Diaspora which followed the capture of Jerusalem by Titus, important Jewish colonies were founded in all the great cities of the Mediterranean and also in Mesopotamia." [17]

"The Diaspora which followed the capture of Jerusalem by Titus" . . . the Mesopotamian or Egyptian Diaspora of A.D. 70—before so dazzling a corroboration there is obviously nothing to do but yield. What fame and fortune for a theological myth—to have the endorsement of the academy, in addition to that of the Church, and to receive what today is the highest official recognition: the palm of the Institute!

4

The historical reality is that the Dispersion began more than five hundred years before the Christian era.

It is time we turned to the second part of our study—the Dispersion in its historical reality, insofar as that reality may be determined from the facts and the documents, as described in the most serious and scholarly historical works.

Considered from the standpoint of objective history alone, with no theological bias, the Dispersion of Israel emerges as a phenomenon of unprecedented scope and complexity: it extends over many centuries, both before and after the birth of Jesus, but principally before. Its causes, its characteristics, its aspects, are extraordinarily diverse. For this reason it is impossible to retrace its principal phases without risking a dangerous oversimplification.

According to A. Causse,[18] a biblical text which seems to be historically sound enables us to go back to the time of Ahab, King of Israel in the ninth century B.C. The Hebrew people, who have always been a prolific group—a fact recognized since antiquity—emigrated at this time to the Syrian city of Damascus, a section of which was set aside for them. It is probable that from the eighth century on they also emigrated to Egypt; in spite of the Exodus, the Hebrews did not harbor unpleasant memories of that fertile land; rather, it held an irresistible attraction for them all through classical times.

However, the Dispersion does not begin to take on any magnitude until after the successive destruction of the two little Hebrew states—the Kingdom of Israel, by the Assyrian Sargon in 722, and the Kingdom of Judah, by the Chaldean Nebuchadnezzar in 586. Not the final episode alone, but each of the invasions, each of the conquests, was

marked by more or less massive deportations to
Mesopotamia, and also by the flight of frightened
populations into Egypt. The people deported to
Mesopotamia, once settled on the lands that had
been assigned them, seem to have adjusted rather
quickly to their fate and to have become farmers,
artisans, and merchants. (This would seem to indicate that human cruelty has advanced somewhat
since the "cruel" Assyrians. Of those deported by
our contemporaries, the Nazis, how many came
back?) Fifty years later, when Cyrus, the new
Persian conqueror, allowed the Palestinian exiles
to return to their own country—to the Promised
Land, the Holy Land—it appears that only a minority accepted the offer and made the journey
back; the majority chose to remain in the land of
exile, which proves that they were not too unhappy
there. So that after this time, let us say a little
over five hundred years before Christ, besides
their homeland in Palestine, newly built around the
restored Temple, the Hebrew people had two other
main places of residence: Mesopotamia (especially
Babylonia) and Egypt. And there were still other
migrations—across the vast Persian Empire, into
Arabia, and among the islands of the eastern Mediterranean, for example. Thus, as early as the
middle of the first millennium B.C., there had occurred a major Diaspora.

Why, one wonders, were these little groups of

Hebrews not absorbed into the human environment where circumstances had placed them? Why did they survive so many hardships, and even prosper, in foreign lands? This is another momentous question, worthy of a separate study, which cannot be avoided and deserves an answer, however brief—a twofold answer, in fact. For we may assume as extremely probable, if not certain, that a portion of these emigrated or deported populations were in fact absorbed by the surrounding environment: Have we not lost track of the ten tribes of Israel? And must we not conclude from this that at least a certain number of the people deported from Israel were swallowed up in the population of Assyria? As for the others—especially those of the Kingdom of Judah, the Judeans—it was their religious faith, their loyalty to Yahwism, and the fiery eloquence of inspired prophets like Ezekiel and the second Isaiah that enabled them to remain apart, tightly grouped in communities of their own. Separatism by divine commandment is taught by the Bible: "For I the Lord am holy, and have separated you from the peoples, that you should be mine," God says in Leviticus 20:26. This religious separatism, by divine and sacerdotal commandment, was to be the spiritual basis of the Diaspora, the scattering of Israel outside Palestine.

5

The Dispersion of Israel saw a great expansion after the conquests of Alexander and the Hellenization of the Orient (4th–2nd centuries B.C.).

The second and most important phase of the Diaspora corresponds to what historians call the Hellenistic period, dating from the conquests of Alexander the Great to the Roman conquest, or from the end of the fourth century to the second century B.C. During this period the Diaspora assumes a new magnitude and takes in the whole Mediterranean East, as well as the Asiatic Near East.

What has objective history to say about this period? Not very much, and that little, rather bizarre at times. In the excellent series, *L'évolution de l'humanité,* founded and for many years directed by the historian Henri Berr (a Jew), I have consulted the volume entitled *L'impérialisme macédonien et l'hellénisation de l'Orient.* It is the contribution of one Pierre Jouguet, an able historian, of whom another able historian writes that "his entire *oeuvre* is a model of lucidity and scru-

pulous care." [19] Here is what M. Jouguet has to
say about Judaism at the time of Alexander: "Alexander . . . must have been sympathetic to the
Jews. The latter, who were insinuating themselves
everywhere, were beginning to be an international
power. . . . There were Jewish communities in
Egypt. . . ." And further on, the author, remark-
ing "how greedily speculators of all nationalities
pounced on Egypt," adds, "In this world so eager
to become rich, it is certain that from the beginning the Jews played their role"—the implication
clearly being, their role as greedy speculators.[20]

"The historian depends first of all on his
sources," M. Jouguet sagely declares. One wonders on what sources he himself relies in asserting
that at the time of Alexander the Jews "were
beginning to be an international power"—on what
hoary "Protocol of the Elders of Zion," the
original of which must have been forged by some
anti-Semite. But what follows clears up the mystery: he refers, naturally, to their financial power.
Has he not already stated that "from the time of
Xerxes"—that is, the first third of the fifth century B.C.—"the Jews were already becoming the
bankers of the world"?[21] We are still waiting
(and I am afraid we shall have a long wait) for
the "sources," the texts supporting these impres-
sive, erroneous, and deliberately misleading statements.

As for the manner in which "the Jews insinu-

ated themselves everywhere" during this period,
we can try to determine what it was. In the first
place, as slaves. Being sold as slaves in all the
markets of the East is undoubtedly one way—although an involuntary one—of "insinuating one-
self everywhere." In fact, it so happens that after
the death of Alexander, and during the continual
wars waged by his successors—notably the two
great Hellenistic powers, the Egyptian monarchy
of the Lagides (or Ptolemies) and the Syrian
monarchy of the Seleucids—Palestine, because of
her location, often served as a battlefield and
passed back and forth from one ruler to the other;
hence the devastation, the slave-making forays, and
the sale of thousands of Judean prisoners on the
slave markets. Well-educated, intelligent, and
industrious for the most part, these Judean slaves
usually succeeded in purchasing their freedom;
aided in this by their fellow believers, they
strengthened the Jewish communities of the Diaspora, or they formed new communities.

Another method of "insinuation": Because the
Judeans in general had a reputation for being
good pioneers, good clearers of land, as well as
good soldiers and loyal servants, the sovereigns
of Hellenistic times employed them—as the Egyptian Pharaohs had previously done—either to
form colonies which were at once agricultural and
military [22] or to populate the countless new cities

they were building all over the East in imitation
of Alexander—whose marvelous creation, Alexandria, had become overnight the greatest com-
mercial and cultural center of the East. (Alexandria, a city half Greek and half Jewish, was the
scene of a bitter economic rivalry which was to
make it the principal source of pagan anti-Semitism.) The Lagides and Seleucids transported,
rather than deported, their Judean subjects by the
thousands into various parts of their empire,
primarily into frontier regions.

Antiochus III, the Great, wrote to the satrap of
Lydia: "I determined to transport two thousand
Jewish families . . . from Mesopotamia and Babylonia to the fortresses and most important
places . . . and I know that they have had the testimony of my forefathers to their good faith and
eagerness to do as they are asked." [23] In the next
generation, Demetrius I, another Seleucid, wrote
to the Maccabean Jonathan, offering to enroll
30,000 men in his army and his private guard. The
offer was declined, but it would appear to prove
that, especially at the time of the Maccabeans and
their victories, Judea served as a market place for
soldiers, just as Switzerland did at the beginning
of our own era, after its victories over the Burgun-
dian army of Charles the Bold. There were also
Judeans in the Egyptian armies; some are even
known to have "insinuated" themselves into the

supreme command. In return for his good services, one of these Jewish generals, Onias, received from Ptolemy VI the gift of a disaffected Egyptian temple at Leontopolis, which thenceforth for over two hundred years was devoted to the worship of Yahweh.

The men of Judea were not only farmers and soldiers, but also merchants and artisans. In the cities, and notably in Alexandria, they carried on all the urban occupations, including that of banking (why not?); but there is nothing to indicate that they were particularly well known at this period as "moneylenders," as is maintained by Father J. M. Lagrange,[24] Pierre Jouguet, and the rest. It seems more likely that they were known as administrators, comptrollers, and accountants, since they seem to have played a major role in the financial administration of Egypt; they also held in that country the "guardianship of the rivers," which would appear to have been equivalent to a force of customs inspectors.[25] M. Jouguet, true to a formula that seems to admit of more prejudices than scruples, writes again: "They insinuated themselves into all the offices, at almost every level of the hierarchy, and they eagerly accepted financial posts." And military posts just as eagerly. Why is this not mentioned? And perhaps all these responsibilities were entrusted to them not because they "insinuated themselves"—in other words,

through conniving—but because their capabilities,
their merits, and their loyalty inspired confidence.

6

*With the Roman Conquest and the
founding of the great Roman Empire,
the Diaspora expanded to include the
whole Mediterranean world.*

The third great phase of the Diaspora, which
followed closely on the second, coincides with the
Roman conquest of the Mediterranean and occidental world, the founding of the great Roman
Empire, and the establishment of a *pax romana*
which lasted for several centuries, leaving so many
noble monuments and also such profound regrets.
This third and last phase dates from the second
century A.D., or the beginning of the Christian
empire. One might even argue that this is not the
final phase, since it omits the subsequent expansion of Judaism beyond Romanized and Christian-
ized regions, primarily into Berber Africa.[26]
The *pax romana* resulted in a tremendous
growth of economic activity and trade between the
oriental and occidental worlds, from one end of

the Mediterranean to the other. The Orient, an older civilization, richer and better equipped for trade, played the dominant role. Like the Greeks and the Syrians, those people, who were later to be called "Jews" and who were known at that time as Judeans (*Ioudaïoi* in Greek, *Judaei* in Latin), were scattered throughout the Western world: Italy, Gaul, the Rhine valley, Spain, the Maghreb. However, the sale of slaves continued to be one of the major causes of the Diaspora; for although the Maccabean—or Hasmonean—dynasty had been the ally of Rome, when the heavy Roman rule was later imposed on the Orient, the people of Judea did not submit to it gracefully, but soon emerged in the empire as a seditious people, quick to rebel, and troublesome in the extreme. After the Greek armies, then, the Roman legions came to Palestine to force them to listen to reason: the capture of Jerusalem by Pompey in 63 B.C. resulted in the sale of thousands of prisoners in the Roman slave market. There already existed a Jewish community in Rome; reinforced by freed slaves, it grew rapidly and before long had assumed an important place in Roman life, both public and private.

With this new colony of the Diaspora, as with all the others, it was the force of religious convictions and customs that kept it apart. Instead of its being absorbed by its pagan milieu, what happened was just the reverse: it was the Judeans who

tended to encroach upon pagan culture by means of
an impassioned and successful proselytism. Thus
each community of the Diaspora was augmented
by converts recruited from the inhabitants of the
country, not to mention a certain number, sometimes quite large, of "God-fearing" pagan sympathizers—those who had not gone so far as to
accept circumcision in order to become acknowledged members of the Jewish community. This is
a phenomenon of major importance, which alters
the whole complexion of the Diaspora, and which
is later to play a significant role in the propaga-
tion of the Christian faith.

Such was the situation before the coming of
Christ. *The Diaspora was a fait accompli.* Its importance was recognized by the Greek geographer
Strabon, a contemporary of the first Roman emperor, Augustus. Describing Cyrenaica, where the
Ptolemies had sent thousands of Judeans, so that
the latter comprised a considerable portion of the
population, Strabon observes: "This people has
already made its way into every city, and it is not
easy to find any place in the habitable world which
has not received this nation and in which it has not
made its power felt." [27] It is very difficult to spec-
ify with any hope of accuracy the numerical
strength of the Jewish population in the Roman
Empire at this time, the beginning of the Christian
era. The estimates vary from one historian to the
next, the most likely figure being between six and

seven million, including two million in Jewish
Palestine. Since the total population of the Empire
at this period barely exceeded sixty million, the
relative importance of the Jewish element was
thus much greater than it is today, even in countries like the United States, where the Jewish population is now larger than anywhere else in the
world. The historian S. W. Baron estimates that
in the eastern provinces of the Empire there must
have been almost twenty Jews in every hundred of
the population.[28]

Together with Palestine and Syria, Egypt and
Mesopotamia continued to be the leading centers
of Jewish population. Alexandria was at once the
greatest Greek city and the greatest Jewish city.
More than a million Jews lived in Babylonia and
in other areas outside of Roman domination.

7

*If the Dispersion of Israel consider-
ably antedates* A.D. *70, can it be said to
have been accomplished at that date?
No. History will not allow it.*

The brief history we have just outlined indicates
rather clearly that it is a notorious blunder—above

all for a member of the French Institute—to date
the Dispersion of Israel from the year 70, or the
capture of Jerusalem by Titus.

Of course many writers are well enough informed not to make this mistake. But there are
many others whom one would expect to know better
and who do not. And how many are there, from
Karl Barth to Marcel Braunschwig—not to mention the Brauns, Fessards, and Prats—who know
the ancient history of the Diaspora inside out, but
surrendering more or less unconsciously to the
force of a two-thousand-year-old tradition (taught
in theological schools), maintain that the year 70
marks the fatal moment of the event, the final and
definitive Dispersion.

How deeply rooted such convictions can be is
further illustrated by a barb recently aimed at me
by one of the Catholic critics of *Jésus et Israël:*
"To confuse the Diaspora with the final dispersion
foretold in Luke 21:24 is frankly laying it on a
bit thick. . . ." [29] This good Father is so shocked
by my bad faith that he stoops to vulgarity.

So we must teach him another lesson in exegesis
and history. For is it not "laying it on even
thicker" to force Scripture and history to say
things they do not say, and to continue to force the
Christian public to believe them?

First, the exegesis. What does Jesus foretell in
Luke 21:24? (He is referring specifically to Jerusalem: "But when you see Jerusalem surrounded

by armies . . .'') ''For . . . they will fall by the
edge of the sword, and will be led away captive
among all nations; and Jerusalem will be trodden
down by the Gentiles, until the times of the Gentiles
are fulfilled.'' Not a word of this passage implies
total or final dispersion. Jerusalem and Judea
devastated, Jews killed and taken prisoner, the
seizure of Jerusalem by the Gentiles: such are
Jesus' prophecies, and nothing more.

And such also is the evidence of history. Not one
good source suggests, as we are always being assured, that Palestinian Judaism, routed for good
and all by the Roman conqueror in 70, from that
time forth ceased to exist. It sustained terrible
losses. According to Flavius Josephus, an historian
who took part in that war and survived it, 1,100,000
died and 97,000 were taken prisoner, to be sold in
the slave markets and eventually to swell the ranks
of the Diaspora.[30] But a massacre is not the same
as a dispersion. After the year 70, Palestinian
Judaism survived as before. We have irrefutable
proof of its survival in the outbreak under the
reign of the great emperor Hadrian, some sixty
years later (132–135), of a second Judean war,
just as bloody and unremitting as the first. To
have carried out this achievement, to have held the
armies of the vast Roman Empire in check for
three years at the height of its power—who can
possibly deny it?—there must surely have been in

Judea more than a handful of rebels. The uprising
of the Jews of Palestine was of such scope and
violence that according to historian Dion Cassius
"the whole world trembled because of it." [31]

One alternative remains: that the final Dispersion should be dated not from 70 but from 135,
after the second Judean war. Some good historians
take this point of view. One such is Ernest Renan:
"From this moment Israel no longer had a homeland, but began that wandering existence which
was to distinguish her for centuries in the astonished eyes of the world." [32] The most recent Catholic chronicler of Jesus and Israel, Professor Ricciotti of the University of Rome, is so impressed
with this solution that he adopts it himself: "From
that day on they have had the wide world for a
home, and their own hearts for a temple." [33] Fine
language, but more eloquent than accurate, and of
a sort to lead a credulous public into error. Not in
135, any more than in 70, were the people of Judea
driven out of this country and forever scattered. A
land horribly devastated; a population shockingly
reduced; thousands upon thousands of prisoners,
leading to an unprecedented drop in prices on the
slave market; all entrance to Jerusalem, their holy
city, forbidden the Judeans—here is the sum total
of the disaster—but there is no definitive dispersion. Once again, Palestinian Judaism survives.

For a long time to come it has lost its military and numerical strength, but it has retained all its spiritual vitality. In the rabbinical schools of Jabneh, and later of Usha, Sepphoris, and Tiberias, it is at this time that the oral tradition is being set down in writing: first in the form of the Mishna, then in its commentary, the Gemara, the whole comprising the Talmud (the so-called Jerusalem Talmud, for a parallel effort was taking place from the second to the fifth centuries in the schools of Mesopotamia, resulting in the Babylonian Talmud). It is inconceivable that the talmudic project could have been carried on for centuries in a land drained of its Jewish population. Indeed, this was not the case, and there is a further proof: Only a few decades after 135—it is impossible to give an exact date, but probably under the reign of Antoninus—there appeared in Palestine a new social institution which in itself bears witness to the enduring importance of Palestinian Judaism, and this is the position of Patriarch, or Ethnarch. Whoever held this position was officially recognized by the Roman authorities as the religious leader of Judaism, and according to the testimony of Origen, was honored as a king.

Q. E. D.: Our demonstration is complete.

8

*No definitive dispersion, but a pro-
gressive impoverishment of Palestinian Judaism—such is the historical
reality which should be obvious to
everyone, theologians and
historians alike.*

The demonstration may be carried a step further. It is not enough to say that no final dispersion occurred either in 70 or in 135; there has
never been a final dispersion. Palestinian Judaism,
weakened by so many wars, rebellions, and massacres, was progressively worn away, like Balzac's
peau de chagrin. During the fourth century, which
saw the founding of the Christian empire, Judaism recovered its strength sufficiently to rebel
against the Emperor Constantine. In the sixth
century it again came to life and rebelled, along
with the Samaritans, against the powerful emperor Justinian, whose government multiplied its
persecutions of the Jews. Each time, there was a
new defeat and a new blood bath. But the indomitable nation did not yield. In the seventh century

they still had enough vitality to form an alliance
with the Persians against the Byzantines, even to
dream of rebuilding a national state, and then to
lend a hand to the new Arab conquerors in over-
throwing a regime which the Christians themselves
barely defended. The Moslem rule seemed mild to
them by comparison, and over a long period they
grew accustomed to it.

It is perhaps to the First Crusade that we must
look, not for a final dispersion, but for the severest
blow dealt to the remnants of Palestinian Judaism
—whether by massacre, by the sale of prisoners
forced into slavery, or by the flight of terrified
populations. Apropos the capture of Jerusalem
by the Crusaders in 1099, I shall merely cite two
curt lines by the historian and teacher René Grousset: "The Crusaders set fire to the synagogue after
having trapped the Jews inside it." [34] Sad prece-
dent of Oradour!

This explains why, when the traveler Benjamin
of Tudela visited Jerusalem around 1170, he found
only a handful of Jewish inhabitants; this race of
bankers (as Jouguet assumes them to be) was
carrying on the more modest profession of dyer.[35]
Ten years later, Abraham the Dyer was the only
one left.[36]

80. Crusade more severe

From this account we may justly conclude that
the traditional Christian doctrine, according to
which the Dispersion of Israel is the punishment

for the Crucifixion, and which occurred in the year 70 of the first century of the Christian era, simply takes no account of historical realities. Thus disowned by history, it becomes no more than a theological myth without the slightest foundation. Therefore, respect for the truth demands that myth's condemnation and disappearance. In such a case it is not history that must come to terms with theology; on the contrary, it is theology that must come to terms with history.

NOTES

1 See *Foi et Vie,* September–October, 1951, p. 563.
2 The principal work dealing objectively with this subject is Marcel Simon's *Verus Israël* (Paris, 1948).
3 Origen, *Against Celsus,* IV: 22. See also *Verus Israël,* p. 90.
4 Saint Augustine, *The City of God,* XVIII: 46.
5 Gregory the Great, *Moralia,* IX: 6, 7, 9; *Homilies,* XXXIX: 1. See also Tiollier, *Saint Grégoire le Grand et les juifs* (Brignais, 1913), p. 19.
6 Sargis d'Aberda (Ethiopian text), in *Patrologia Orientalis,* III, 507.
7 The latest is S. W. Baron's *A Social and Religious History of the Jews* (New York, second edition 1952—).
8 F. M. Braun, *Où en est le problème de Jésus?,* p. 147.
9 Gaston Fessard, *Pax nostra* (Paris, 1936), pp. 201, 202, 206, 207.
10 Ferdinand Prat, *Jésus-Christ* (Paris, fifth ed., 1933), Vol. II, p. 372.
11 Bérard, *Saint Augustin et les juifs* (Besançon, 1913), p. 73; F. Vernet, *Dictionnaire de théologie catholique* (Paris, 1925), VII: 2, col. 1884.

12   F. J.-H. Leenhardt, *L'antisémitisme et le mystère d'Israël* (Geneva, 1929), p. 26.

13   Jean Bosc, "Le mystère d'Israël," *Réforme,* November 23, 1946.

14   Karl Barth, "La réponse chrétienne au problème juif," *Foi et Vie,* May–June 1951, pp. 265, 266. Discussed by the author in the issue for September–October 1951, pp. 559–563.

15   For the sources of these quotations, see Father Démann's *La catéchèse chrétienne et le peuple de la Bible* (Paris, 1952), pp. 155–160.

16   Marcel Braunschwig, *Le vrai visage d'Israël* (Paris, 1948), pp. 41, 105.

17   A. Fliche, and V. Martin, *Histoire de l'Eglise,* Vol. V, p. 108.

18   A. Causse, *Les dispersés d'Israël* (Paris, 1929), pp. 9–23.

19   A. Aymard, in *Revue des études anciennes,* 1947, p. 322.

20   Pierre Jouguet, *La vie municipale dans l'Egypte romaine,* pp. 114, 379. The author does add, it is true, that the majority (of these scavengers) were Greeks.

21   *Ibid.,* p. 13.

22   The oldest known example is the Jewish colony of Elephantine, concerning which existing documents date to the fifth century B.C., but which goes back as far as the sixth and possibly even the seventh century B.C.

23   Quoted by the Jewish historian Flavius Josephus in *Jewish Antiquities,* XII: 3: 4, and generally regarded as authentic. (From the Ralph Marcus translation, Loeb Classical Library. London, 1943; Vol. VII, pp. 77–78.) See Juster, *Les juifs dans l'Empire romain,* Vol. II, p. 268, n. 1.

24   J. M. Lagrange, *Le Judaïsme avant Jésus-Christ* (Paris, 1931), p. 520. *Contra* Dom Duesberg, *Le roi Hérode* (1932), p. 251: "Only one occupation was unknown to them at the time, that of banking"—likewise an extreme statement, since there were Jewish banks in those days, notably at Alexandria.

25   See Juster, *op. cit.,* Vol. II, pp. 256–257.

26   See Marcel Simon, "Le Judaïsme berbère," *Revue d'Histoire et de Philosophie religieuse,* 1946.

27   Flavius Josephus, *Jewish Antiquities,* XIV: 7: 2. (From

the Ralph Marcus translation, Vol. VII, p. 509.) See Juster, *op. cit.,* Vol. I, p. 180.

28   S. W. Baron, *A Social and Religious History of the Jews,* Vol. I.

29   Abbé Tissier, mimeographed lessons (No. 220, p. 5).

30   Flavius Josephus, *The Jewish War,* IV : 9 : 3.

31   Théodore Reinach, *Textes . . . relatifs au judaïsme,* p. 199.

32   Ernest Renan, *L'Eglise chrétienne,* p. 226.

33   Giuseppe Ricciotti, *History of Israel* (French edition), Vol. II, p. 581.

34   René Grousset, *Histoire des Croisades,* Vol. I (Paris, 1934), p. 168.

35   *The Itinerary of Benjamin of Tudela* (London, 1907).

36   S. W. Baron, *op. cit.,* Vol. IV.

II

THE DEGENERATE STATE OF
JUDAISM AT THE TIME
OF JESUS

1

Another theological contention, invented, reinforced, and propagated for hundreds of years, is that at the time of Jesus the religion of Israel was mere legalism without a soul.

The degenerate state of Judaism at the dawn of the Christian era is another of the favorite themes of the teaching of contempt. According to its doctrines, which are so deep-rooted even today, the religion of Israel, desiccated, ossified, reduced to

mere formalism and ritual, was at the time of Jesus
no more than legalism without a soul, without
fervor, without any true aspiration toward God.

This contention has its source in the earliest
Judeo-Christian controversies over the Torah—
the Law of Moses—and its observance. The Christian apologists maintained that with the coming of
Christ, the Law had been fulfilled and superseded.
They taught that the Jews were attached to the
letter and not the spirit of the law because they
were "carnal" beings, blinded by Satan, incapa-
ble of understanding the real meaning of their
own Scriptures.

During the fourth century, the first century of
the Christian empire, the Church Fathers return
constantly to this theme. Saint Jerome does not
hesitate to declare of the Jews that "their prayers
and psalms are like the inarticulate cries of ani-
mals." Saint John Chrysostom, preaching in 386
at Antioch, where there were still a number of
Christians sympathetic to the old Law, rails bit-
terly against the "carnal" Jews (those "unclean
and savage beasts"), against the synagogue ("the
house of the devil"), and against the Jewish religion, which is by now no more than "a mockery, a
parody, and a disgrace." [1]

Some two hundred years later, Pope Gregory
the Great, although infinitely more humane in his
treatment of the Jews, and more restrained in the
tone of his writings, remains inflexible on this

point: "[The Jewish people] have been faithful only to the letter of the divine commandments. . . . A people more dedicated to the world than to the truth . . . who had but a fleshly understanding of the Incarnation of God, and refused to see in Him anything but a man."

From this to the assertion that Judaism had degenerated into mere "superstition," and at the time of the coming of Christ was a "fallen" religion, is only a step, and it was not long in being taken. In the sixteenth century, at the time of the Reformation, this seemed as obvious to the Reformed Church as it had to the Church of Rome:

"Matters had come to such a pass with these people, so great and so widespread were the abuses, so thoroughly had the high priests extinguished the pure light of doctrine through their negligence or malice, that there scarcely remained any respect for the Law." (Calvin, *Commentaries on the New Testament,* I, p. 155)

Oddly enough, it is in our own time, when historical research has made possible a better understanding of the true nature of pre-Christian Judaism, and of the vitality it has never ceased to demonstrate, that the theme of "the degenerate state of Judaism" has reached its full magnitude, both in the writings of theologians and in scholarly publications.

A few typical examples may be selected from various cultural and educational levels. Beginning with the highest, a quotation from *The Son of God,*

the work of an outstanding German Catholic theologian, Karl Adam, well known and widely read
throughout the Catholic world:

"How could there have emerged from a world
which was falling in ruins—a world of ossified belief in the letter, of a narrow-minded caste spirit
and materialistic piety, a world of skepticism,
doubt, and libertinism—a human nature so incom-
parably pure, so God-united and holy and gracious,
so inwardly free and genuine as his?"[2]

The same idea is echoed by a passage from a
Protestant theologian, Gunther Dehn, taken from
*Le Fils de Dieu: commentaire à l'Evangile de
Marc,* the first volume (published in 1936) in a
series of French studies which are no less well
known: "For hundreds of years, Israel was as
though abandoned by God; the living God of their
fathers had become a God remote and inaccessible.
Schools, teachers, the observance of the law, religious zeal, all this had survived . . ."

The same idea was expressed briefly by a monk
who was interviewed in February, 1948, by the
Catholic writer Julien Green. "Israel worshiped
God only in a conventional manner"—a widespread, devastating, but ignorant opinion.

From such books for adult laymen and members
of the clergy, Catholic and Protestant, let us turn
to the manuals of religious instruction for young
people. The remarkable investigation conducted
between 1950 and 1952 by Father Démann and the
greatly lamented Renée Bloch,[3] and published as

La catéchèse chrétienne et le peuple de la Bible,[4]
provides us with innumerable statements of this
kind.

"The religious life of the Jewish people, led
astray by the Pharisees, was on the road to deca-
dence. . . ."

"The religious life of the Jews was reduced at
the time of Jesus to a mere external formalism. . . ."

"Nothing remains of the great religion of Abraham, David, Moses, and the Prophets; save for a
narrow ritualism, it is no more than a national
cult, which reduces the idea of God to the scale of
this stiff-necked and tormented people. . . . Cor-
rupt priests, scribes copying out formulas, hardhearted and hypocritical Pharisees . . ."

"The people to whom Jesus addressed himself . . . sought to find happiness in silver and
gold, in base sensuality, in vain display, dispute
and revenge. Their only desires: the enjoyment
of riches, pleasure and power . . ."[5]

Most of the handbooks heap blame on the Pharisees, whose religious influence was great:

"The scribes and Pharisees had not the slightest
concern for moral or spiritual purity. . . . To a
formalism that was strict and detailed to the point
of absurdity, they brought the most consummate
pride and hypocrisy." (M. Lepin, professor at the
Major Seminary at Lyon, in his Introduction to
L'Evangile de Notre-Seigneur Jésus-Christ, 1934)

"The Pharisees . . . are hypocrites, their religion is a farce, they overload the law of God with countless minutiae and elaborate rites . . . but underneath, their hearts are full of pride, ambition, and malice." (Sisters of Bernadette, *Sainte Bible ou Histoire sainte,* No. 4, p. 73)

Among all these books of instruction there are undoubtedly exceptions—authors who are better informed, more impartial—but they are still only the exception. The majority cling to the tradition of prejudice, whose accusations, Father Démann has observed, "correspond neither to the data of history . . . nor to the needs of religious instruction." What is it, then, that keeps ecclesiastical authorities from condemning them?

2

Once again, historical reality belies the main arguments of traditional teaching, in attesting to the vitality of the religious life of Israel at this period.

Here, we must make a sharp distinction between the years before and after 1950, for in that year the data provided by the miraculous discovery of the Dead Sea Scrolls first began to be understood. That discovery profoundly revived, altered, indeed revolutionized the study of pre-Christian Judaism, and therefore the study of the origins of Christianity.

Even before the discovery, there had been a number of works, for example those of Father J. M. Lagrange and Father Joseph Bonsirven in France, which helped us to form a clearer, more accurate image of Judaism before and during the time of Jesus. I shall merely retrace here in simplified form the picture I outlined in *Jésus et Israël,* written between 1943 and 1946, and published in 1948.[6]

One who examines the facts objectively, without prejudice or apologetic zeal, is obliged to admit at the outset that in the traditional Christian teachings, however misleading as a whole, there are particles of truth embedded in a mass of untruths.

Thus, one may say of pre-Christian Judaism that the legalism and formalism of the scribes, the Doctors of the Law, though possibly justifiable and even reasonable, was also not without its dangers and excesses.

One may say that there was hypocrisy, that there was false piety on the part of the Pharisees; it is denounced in the Talmud as well as in the Gospels. But is not religious bigotry to be found in all times and all churches? Is Tartuffe a Jew?

It may be said that there was in Judea, at Jeru-

salem, a harsh and arrogant priestly oligarchy
such as that of Annas and Caiphas—a group hos-
tile to anyone who appeared to threaten the established order from which it was benefiting. But is not
the Zechariah of the Gospel sufficient proof in the
eyes of the Christians that there were still warm-
hearted, genuinely devout men in the Jewish
priesthood?

It may be said that there was a messianic rest-
lessness from which temporal motives, especially
anti-Roman feelings, were not absent; but is it so
astonishing that a nation subjected to foreign rule
and foreign occupation should yearn so passionately, so fiercely, for its independence?

What may not be said, what no one has any
right to say, is that formalism, ritualism, hypocrisy, arrogance, and worldliness were the essence,
the sum total, of Judaism or of Pharisaism. The
most valid historical research has incontestably
shown the enduring vitality and profundity of the
religious life of Israel.

Let us give a few of the most striking proofs of
this. First of all, from the second century B.C. until
the beginning of the Christian era, there is a
wealth of Jewish religious literature, both canonical and extracanonical. The former includes the
Book of Daniel; the latter, the First and Second
Books of the Maccabees,[7] the Testaments of the
Twelve Patriarchs, the Book of Jubilees, the Book

of Enoch, and the Odes and Psalms of Solomon, among a great many others.

Next there is the stubborn, energetic, and furious resistance of Jewish piety to the constant encroachment of the paganism of the conquerors. The intolerance of Greek paganism brought on the heroic and eventually victorious uprising of the Maccabeans. Against Roman paganism the Jewish rebellions were ultimately unsuccessful, but in their struggle, spiritual and religious motives were inextricably mingled with temporal ones.

Nor can we ignore the remarkable evolution of the Synagogue, that place of gathering and prayer which was a unique and original institution in the ancient world. Its spiritualized worship, stripped of all ritualism, consisted of prayers, hymns, reading, and comment on the sacred texts. It was there that Jesus himself, according to the testimony of the Gospels, never ceased teaching. Indeed, that the Synagogue is the "mother of the Christian church and the Mohammedan mosque" is admitted by the Christian writers themselves: it was, according to Adolphe Lods, "the first attempt to realize the ideal of worship in spirit." [8]

The spread of Jewish religious influence in the pagan world, in Rome and throughout the Roman Empire, is another compelling indication of vitality. The weekly Sabbatical rest began to become a popular institution, and each synagogue gathered about it an increasing number of sympathizers;

some "proselytes" became members of the Jewish community through circumcision, others were merely Judaizers or "God-fearing" pagans like the centurion in Luke 7: 1–10.

The continual enrichment of religious life through the adoption of new beliefs, for example in the resurrection of the dead and the last judgment, is also relevant. The Pharisees, who are the men of the Halakah, the oral tradition which elucidates the written Law of the Torah, made a major contribution to this enrichment.

One has only to recall some of the sayings of the Jewish sages in order to rectify the caricature which is still so prevalent in Christian teaching: "Do not do to others what you would not have others do to you," says Hillel. "This is the whole Law; the rest is but commentary." And another: "Whether you accomplish much or little does not matter, provided your heart is turned toward heaven." The vindication of the Pharisees in the eyes of history has long since been accomplished.

What else, then, should be mentioned? The strange mystical and apocalyptic current issuing from the preaching of the Prophets, the vitality and diversity of messianic aspirations which, the texts show clearly, are far from a preoccupation with "earthly things"; the messianic expectation was an ardent anticipation of "the Kingdom of Heaven" in pietist circles such as "the poor of Israel."

By way of example, let us cite a single extract
from the seventeenth of the Psalms of Solomon
(first century B.C.), which expresses the messianic
hope that stirred the Pharisees:

The awaited Messiah, this "Son of David,"

. . . shall not put his trust in horse and rider and bow,
Nor shall he multiply for himself gold and silver for war,
Nor shall he gather confidence from [?] a multitude [?]
    for the day of battle.
The Lord Himself is his king, the hope of him that is
    mighty through [his] hope in God.
All nations [shall be] in fear before him,
For he will smite the earth with the word of his mouth
    for ever.[9]

3

*The discovery of the Dead Sea Scrolls
has caused a spectacular revival of the
Essenes, one of the principal Jewish
sects at the time of Jesus.*

Still another proof of the vitality of pre-Christian Judaism, which so many Christian authors
dare to refer to as a degenerate and "fallen" religion, is the multiplicity of the various sects that

were marginal to official Judaism, although not necessarily in conflict with it.

Now here is the miracle: one of these sects, a rather obscure one, which has remained mysterious in certain respects, has been suddenly brought to life. How? Through one of the most astonishing discoveries of our time, the discovery of certain very ancient manuscripts hidden in the caves of the Judean desert, not far from the Dead Sea. The discovery took place in 1947, purely by chance— with a Bedouin looking for a lost goat—but several years passed before the significance of the manuscripts was recognized and the clandestine searches of the Bedouins gave way to the systematic exploration of the caves of the region by qualified scholars. Since 1952 the field of investigation has expanded considerably, and has been enormously fruitful. During this period, archeological excavations near the initial site at Qumran have brought to light the ruins of a communal building as well as the cemetery of the community, consisting of more than a thousand graves.

It is highly probable, and most of the experts are agreed, that the manuscripts and fragments of manuscripts that have been found are the remnants of the library of the Essenes, a monastic sect; the caves probably served as a hiding place at the time of the first Judean war (66–70), when the approach of the Roman legions forced the Essenes to abandon their monastery and flee.

These discoveries have given rise to innumerable investigations, publications, and controversies.
Among the most important we may mention A.
Dupont-Sommer, *The Essene Writings from Qumran* (Oxford, 1961); Millar Burrows, *The Dead
Sea Scrolls* (New York, 1955) and *More Light on
the Dead Sea Scrolls* (New York, 1958); J. T.
Milik, *Ten Years of Discovery in the Wilderness
of Judea* (London, 1959); and a good résumé of the
subject in Chapter III of Marcel Simon's little
book, *Les sectes juives au temps de Jésus* (Paris,
1960).

Among the manuscripts that have been found
and published thus far, some are biblical texts,
notably the Book of Isaiah almost in its entirety.
To give an idea of their importance, it is enough
to say that these manuscripts are approximately a
thousand years older than the oldest biblical manuscripts previously known. Other works, utterly
unknown until the time of the discovery, have to
do with the organization and doctrine of the Qumran Jewish sect, which has now been identified with
the Essenes. Of these, the four principal manuscripts are an almost complete text of the rules and
practices of the Community, entitled "The Manual of Discipline"; a commentary on the prophet
Habakkuk; a collection of thanksgiving hymns;
and a book called "The War of the Sons of Light
and the Sons of Darkness." In this connection,
mention should be made of a manuscript discov-

ered fifty years earlier (1896) in a synagogue in old Cairo, known as the Damascus Document; it had a close connection with the newly discovered writings, and without them its obscurity seemed all but impenetrable.

The Essenes were not unknown to history. Jewish writers of the first century, including Philo and Josephus, as well as pagan authors (notably Pliny the Elder), had written about them at some length. It was known that the sect was about a hundred and fifty years old at the time of Jesus, and that it was an authentic religious order, to which admission was granted only after a long novitiate, consisting of a gradual initiation into certain secret doctrines. Though essentially Jewish, it seems to have been affected by Greek (Pythagorean) and Persian influences. Members of the order followed strict rules of purity, chastity, temperance, silence, and work; above all, they were pledged to absolute poverty, surrendering all their worldly goods to the Community. They also engaged in charitable and fraternal works. With respect to the Torah they were Jews of the strictest observance, stricter even than the Pharisees, but they did not approve of the sacrificial rites of the Temple. Their rigorous asceticism was not limited to a trifling minority, for many thousands of Jews embraced it voluntarily. The center of the Community, the mother house, was located near the Dead Sea, but there were branches in almost

every town. So much for this "carnal" people,
this religion enslaved by "worldly concerns." In
spite of the mystery in which it was shrouded, the
sect emerges as a center of spiritual life, of intense
piety, and of mystical asceticism.

Oddly enough, the name of the Essenes is never
mentioned in the Gospels, whereas the Pharisees
are frequently under discussion. For many years
an attempt was made to establish a link between
the Essenes and Christianity—notice was taken of
obvious affinities between them—but in the absence
of any documentary evidence, the thesis was eventually abandoned by the best-informed historians
and biblical scholars.

4

*Thanks to recent discoveries, we can
now have an accurate understanding
of the high religious aspirations of
this Jewish sect, whose guide was an
inspired priest, the Teacher
of Righteousness.*

Today, now that our knowledge of the Essenian
sect is no longer limited to hearsay—now that it

has, so to speak, come to life before our eyes—what
does it reveal about itself? What is the substance
of its thrilling message from beyond the grave?

First of all, it is the extraordinary revelation of
a powerful religious personality who until now has
remained hidden from the light of history, and
who is still anonymous despite all our investigations: a wise and holy priest reverently referred
to in the documents of the sect as the "Doctor of
the Law," or the "Teacher of Righteousness."
During a period which is still under debate (some
scholars place it at the middle of the second century B.C., others at the beginning of the first), this
saintly personage seems to have become involved
in a struggle with the "Wicked Priest," the "Man
of Lies," who is identified with one or another of
the priest-kings of the Hasmonean dynasty
founded by the Maccabees. At any rate, the
Teacher of Righteousness seems to have been horribly persecuted and threatened during his lifetime, perhaps even put to death; on this point the
texts are open to debate, and we can be sure of
nothing. But "the language of the Mysteries," say
the texts, "was revealed to him by God," as it was
to Moses—even more than to Moses; his teachings,
faithfully recorded, became the basis for the doctrines of the sect, which thenceforth regarded itself
as the "New Covenant," the "Party of God," the
only true Israel, the "true remnant."

Whether or not the Teacher of Righteousness

was revered after his death as "The Lord's Anointed"—that is to say, as the Messiah—is a very controversial question. It seems that the sect believed in the coming of two Messiahs—the "Messiah of Aaron," or Priest-Messiah, and the "Messiah of Israel," or King-Messiah, the Son of David. It must have been as the Messiah of Aaron, the Priest-Messiah, that the Teacher of Righteousness was revered by his followers. Several texts seem to indicate that the Teacher of Righteousness, "God's Chosen One," closely linked to God and by him appointed supreme Judge, was to preside at the Last Judgment. However, on these points some difference of opinion persists. What is certain, what is universally acknowledged, and what seems, moreover, to imply the messianic reputation of the departed Teacher, is the fact that for the members of the "New Covenant," the condition of salvation is no less than faith in the Teacher of Righteousness.

In the Commentary on Habakkuk the author, coming upon the line, "The righteous shall live by his faith," writes, "The explanation of this concerns all those who observe the Law. . . . God will deliver them from the House of Judgment because of their affliction and their faith in the Teacher of Righteousness." [10] Could faith in the person and mission of the Teacher be the condition of salvation, if this person and this mission had an exclusively worldly significance and not an

otherworldly, transcendent one? The very fact
that the Teacher of Righteousness is never called
by name must be regarded as an unusual mark of
veneration, such as is accorded to God himself.
The faithful await his return, "the coming of the
Teacher of Righteousness at the end of days," as
is promised in the Damascus Document.[11]

In the spring of 1944, while I was hiding in the
French village of Berry, Levroux, and working on
the third part of *Jésus et Israël,* I could still subscribe to the opinion that "the idea of a Messiah
who suffered and was put to death was, or seems to
have been, unknown to the Jews at the time of
Jesus. It was he who revealed it and consecrated
it with his blood." The truth unexpectedly revealed
by the Dead Sea Scrolls is that at least a hundred
years before Jesus, thousands of Jews—the men
of the New Covenant, the Essenes—followed a
Teacher who was persecuted, tortured, perhaps
put to death, and who identified himself with the
Servant of God, the Man of Sorrows whose unforgettable portrait has been drawn by the prophet
Isaiah (Isaiah 53).

In the Hymns of Thanksgiving, where the
Teacher of Righteousness appears to be speaking
directly, he does not hesitate to present himself as
the Servant, in Isaiah's sense: "And Thou hast
favored Thy servant with the Spirit of Knowledge
. . . for Thou hast upheld me by Thy might, and
poured out Thy Holy Spirit upon Thy servant." [12]

Like the Servant in Isaiah, the Teacher accepts his
destiny as a hunted, forsaken man, "in bitterness
and incurable anguish," weighed down by suffering and disease, but trusting in the help of God and
full of joy even in his pain: "For . . . I have
loved my judgment and the blows which struck me
were pleasant to me . . . and the scorn of my ad-
versaries has become for me a glorious crown, and
my stumbling, everlasting might." [13]

We are a long way from the fleshly desires
and soulless legalism which continue to be re-
iterated by the traditional Christian teaching of
contempt. For the purity, the nobility, the lofti-
ness of the religious life of the New Covenant, as
it was defined and fixed by the Teacher of Righteousness, and as it comes down to us in the Manual
of Discipline and the Hymns of Thanksgiving, is
an entirely different—but no less compelling—revelation.

Jews of the strictest observance of the Law,
the members of the Community respected all the
commandments of the Torah, and observed all the
prescribed rituals. To this they added the daily
routine of a baptismal bath of purification. But the
Manual of Discipline stresses repeatedly that
purification of the body had no worth in the sight
of God unless it was accompanied by purification
of the heart and mind in accordance with the doctrines of the Teacher.

Whoever scorns to enter the ways of God in order to walk
   in the stubbornness of his heart . . .
He shall not be absolved by atonement,
nor purified by lustral waters, . . .
Unclean, unclean shall he be
for as long as he scorns the ordinances of God
and allows not himself to be taught by the Community of
   His Council.
For by the Holy Spirit of the Community, in His truth,
shall he be cleansed of all his sins;
and by the Spirit of uprightness and humility
shall his iniquity be atoned.
By his soul's humility towards all the precepts of God
shall his flesh be cleansed
when sprinkled with lustral water
and sanctified in flowing water. . . .[14]

Complete humility before God, total submission
to his will—such was the basic principle of religious life for the New Covenant. But we must let
these beautiful passages speak for themselves, and
listen to what are undoubtedly the very words of
the Teacher of Righteousness:

I will sing in Knowledge,
and my whole lyre shall throb to the Glory of God,
and my lute and harp to the holy Order which He has
   made.

.   .   .   .

At the beginning of every enterprise of my hands or feet
I will bless His Name;

at the beginning of every activity, . . .
I will utter cries of joy unto Him. . . .

.   .   .   .

in the depth of distress, in full desolation,
I will bless Him.

.   .   .   .

and I will lean on His favours every day.
I know that in His hand is judgment of all the living . . .

.   .   .   .

To no man will I render the reward of evil,
with goodness will I pursue each one;

.   .   .   .

For God's truth is the rock of my steps
and His power, the stay of my right hand,
and from the fount of His Righteousness comes my justi-
    fication.

.   .   .   .

For without Thee no way is perfect,
and without Thy will nothing is done. . . .
And there is none other beside Thee
to dispute Thy decision
and to comprehend all Thy holy Thought
and to contemplate the depth of Thy Mysteries

.   .   .   .

And he that is born of woman,
what is his worth before Thee?
Truly, this man was shaped from dust
and his end is to become the prey of worms. . . .
What shall clay reply, the thing which the hand fashions?
What thought [of its Creator] can it comprehend? [15]

Out of his contemplation of the abysmal nothing-
ness which is man compared with the Omnipotence

of the Creator, the Teacher of Righteousness
reached the conclusion which is the pinnacle of his
theology: There was no salvation, no possible justification for man, save by the grace of God.

For is man master of his way?
No, men cannot establish their steps,
for their justification belongs to God,
and from His Hand comes perfection of way. . . .
and without Him nothing is made.

And I, if I stagger,
God's mercies are my salvation for ever;
and if I stumble because of the sin of the flesh,
my justification is in the righteousness of God
which exists for ever.[16]

During a previous debate concerning *Jésus et
Israël,* I was charged with having minimized the
profound antagonism between Jesus and the Pharisees, and even Judaism as a whole. I was told that
the Gospel of Jesus was "a revelation of grace,"
and therefore in direct opposition to any religion,
to the degree that it is "a human attempt at rec-
onciliation with God through obedience, good
works, and piety." The charge was not entirely
fair, even as applied to the Judaism of the Pharisees. "Be not like those servants who serve their
master to receive a reward," counsels a wise
Pharisee doctor (Pirke Avot I, 3). And when it
comes to the Judaism of the New Covenant, to the
teachings of the Teacher of Righteousness, the pas-

sages just quoted only demonstrate with dazzling clarity that more than a hundred years before the birth of Christianity, this Judaism was a religion of grace.

Since this portrait is somewhat brief, I cannot resist adding one more essential stroke: the doctrine of the two Ways, or the two Spirits.

Toward the end of the seventh century B.C., the Persian sage Zarathustra, or Zoroaster, is said to have taught that the world was the scene of a desperate struggle between two Spirits, the Spirit of Good and the Spirit of Evil. All natural and supernatural forces were engaged in this awful and protracted conflict, which would end with the victory of good over evil, of light over darkness.

This lofty idea, coming from the East, seems to have made a deep impression on the elite of Israel. We find echoes of it in the biblical Psalms and Proverbs and in the books of Daniel and Enoch. But it was unknown until recently that it was one of the essential elements of the secret doctrine of the Essenes. We find it explicitly formulated, undoubtedly by the Teacher of Righteousness himself, in the Manual of Discipline:

From the God of Knowledge comes all that is and shall be, and before [beings] were, he established all their design.

.   .   .   .

And He allotted unto man two Spirits; . . .
they are the Spirits of truth and perversity. . . .

Dominion over all the sons of righteousness
is in the hands of the Prince of light;
they walk in the ways of light.
All dominion over the sons of perversity
is in the hand of the Angel of darkness;
they walk in the ways of darkness.

.   .   .   .

For God has allotted these [two spirits] in equal parts
    until the final end,
and has set between their divisions eternal hatred.
An abomination to Truth are the deeds of Perversity,
and an abomination to Perversity are all the ways of
    Truth. . . .[17]

However, we must be on our guard, for the
battle between the Spirits of Good and Evil does
not find expression in this world solely in the conflict between the two warring tribes, the Sons of
Righteousness and the Sons of Perversity. For the
battle is also waged in the heart of every man:

Till now the Spirits of truth and perversity battle in the
    hearts of every man;
[they] walk in Wisdom and Folly.
And according to each man's share of Truth and Right-
    eousness,
so does he hate Perversity.
And according to his portion in the lot of Perversity,
and [according to] the wickedness [which is] in him,
so does he abominate Truth.[18]

And so it will be until the final day determined
by God, "the day of Judgment and Visitation."

On that day, when God causes the Prince of Light
and Truth to triumph over the Angel of Darkness,
those who have allowed themselves to be led astray
by the latter—the Sons of Perversity—will suffer
the most horrible fate, the worst torments, until
"the annihilation by fire of the regions of darkness," while the others, the Sons of Righteousness, will know "all blessings without end"

And the joy of eternal life,
And the crown of glory . . . in the perpetual light.

Such was the vision of Heaven and Hell set
forth by the Teacher of Righteousness.

5

*The discoveries at Qumran have revo-
lutionized not only the history of pre-
Christian Judaism, but likewise that
of the origins of Christianity.*

The more one studies these exciting and mirac-
ulously discovered manuscripts, the more one is
struck by the affinities of form and content, of
style and inspiration, which they exhibit with the
texts of the New Testament and of other Chris-

tian writings dating from the birth of Christianity.
Naturally, the similarities do not cancel out the
differences, and those differences are not minor
but profound. Nevertheless, it is now conceded
that Christianity drew heavily upon this source;
it bears a stamp that is unmistakable.

Thus the history not only of the origins of Christianity but also of its early development appears
in a totally new light. We are still on the thresh-
old of this extraordinary recasting of history,
of the examination of the documents, for the
discoveries have multiplied with such rapidity
that there are still other texts to be deciphered and
published. We are only at the beginning of the
critical studies which are sure to enable us—which
already enable us—to alter or to deepen our understanding of many ideas of long standing.

The discussion ensuing upon the publication of
the first manuscripts discovered at Qumran has
not been entirely free from prejudice and distortion of one sort or another, but it has lately taken
a more strictly objective and scientific tone. Thus
Catholics, after trying to minimize the importance
of the discoveries, have now admitted it frankly:
as, for example, in the essay by Father Jean
Daniélou, S.J., *The Dead Sea Scrolls and Primitive Christianity*. His conclusions should be compared with those of the authors already cited:
André Dupont-Sommer (Chapter XIV, "Essenism
and Christianity"); Marcel Simon (Chapter VI,

"Les sectes juives et le christianisme"); Millar
Burrows (1955, Chapter XV; 1958, Part Two);
and also Duncan Howlett, *The Essenes and Christianity* (New York, 1957). There remain points of
controversy; the discussion is still wide open, and
will be for some time to come.

The first question to arise is, Did Jesus have
any connection with the Essenes? Was he influenced by the teachings of the Teacher of Righteousness?

We know that according to the Gospel tradition, Jesus had a forerunner, John the Baptist.
Now John preached in the Judean desert, not far
from the site of Qumran. He was originally a priest,
as were the leaders of the sect. Like them, he led
an ascetic life, and called for repentance, together with baptism in the waters of the Jordan,
in preparation for the imminence of the Day of
Judgment.

In Matthew 3:2–4 we read: "And saying, Re-
pent, for the kingdom of heaven is at hand. For
this is he who was spoken of by the prophet Isaiah
when he said, 'The voice of one crying in the
wilderness: Prepare the way of the Lord, make
his paths straight.'" Now, in the Manual of Discipline we read as follows: "They [the members
of the Community] shall be separated from . . .
the habitation . . . of perverse men to go into the
desert to prepare the way of 'Him': as it is writ-

ten: In the desert prepare ye the way of . . .
Make straight in the desert a highway for our
God.'' [19]

We may assume that John the Baptist was, if
not one of the Essenes himself, at least influenced
by them, and that through him and through his
disciples, Jesus, when he came from Galilee, was
familiar with the sect and its doctrines. There is
an obvious parallel between the Teacher of Righteousness, who was persecuted and perhaps even
martyred, and Jesus, who was hated by the high
priests, was arrested, fell into the hands of the
Romans, and was crucified. Do not both men apply
to themselves those passages in Isaiah on the Servant of Yahweh and the Man of Sorrows?

But the similarities are outweighed by the differences, especially the following: The ''Teacher''
is a learned priest, and gives priests the highest
place in the New Covenant, whereas Jesus is a
man of the people, an artisan, unimpressed by the
priestly hierarchy. The Teacher is an ascetic, who
prescribes the ascetic life for all members of the
sect, whereas Jesus seems neither to have practiced nor have preached any form of asceticism.
The Teacher organized a closed sect with a secret
doctrine, known only to initiates chosen from
among the wisest and most righteous, whereas
Jesus, ''the people's preacher,'' addresses himself to everyone, even to the ''publicans and sinners,'' and by preference to the simple-hearted,

the "poor in spirit"; the Teacher and his disciples are the strictest of all Jews in observing the commandments of the Torah, whereas Jesus, though he both respects the commandments and teaches respect for them, does so in a more humane and liberal spirit.

Father Daniélou [20] calls our attention to the question raised by Christ after curing a man afflicted with the dropsy on the Sabbath day, to the great outrage of the Pharisees: "Which of you, having an ass or an ox that has fallen into a well, will not immediately pull him out on a sabbath day?" (Luke 14:5) This indicates that the act must have been acceptable according to the customs of the Pharisees. Now, the matter is anticipated in the Rule of the Community, and the answer is in the negative. (XI, 12, and XI, 16) Thus the Pharisees were more liberal than the Essenes, and Jesus was more liberal than either.

Where the influence of the Essenes is evident is in the organization of the first Christian communities, in the wording of the Gospels—especially the Gospel according to John—in some of the Epistles of Saint Paul, and in some of the oldest Christian writings, such as *The Shepherd* of Hermas, which are now attributed to Essenes converted to Christianity. These Essenian converts must have been fairly numerous.

We shall confine ourselves to a few typical examples. In the Acts of the Apostles, 2:42–45, we read, concerning the first Christians: "And they devoted themselves to the apostles' teaching and fellowship, to the breaking of bread and the prayers . . . and had all things in common; and they sold their possessions and goods and distributed them to all, as any had need." Fellowship, breaking of bread, prayers, selling of possessions, common ownership—exactly what is prescribed by the Manual of Discipline.

In John 1:4–5, we read: "In him [the Word of God] was life, and the life was the light of men. The light shines in the darkness, and the darkness has not overcome it." Father Daniélou comments: "Now this is nothing else but the *leitmotif* of Qumran. . . . The Gospel of John is entirely constructed on the theme of the conflict between light and darkness." And we meet it again in the Epistles of Saint Paul, where the "Prince of Darkness" is given the name of Belial, a name much in use at Qumran.[21]

We read in the seventh of the Qumran Hymns of Thanksgiving: "And thou hast . . . established my fabric upon rock; and everlasting foundations serve me for my ground and all my walls are a tried rampart which nothing can shake."[22] It is impossible not to hear the echo in Matthew 16:18: ". . . and on this rock I will build my church, and the powers of death shall not prevail against it."

In the Didache, the first Christian prayer book,

the catechism of preparation for baptism is based
on the Essenian catechism of the Two Ways in the
Manual of Discipline. In *The Shepherd* of Hermas
the moral teachings are based on the doctrine of
the Two Spirits.[23]

These are only a few examples among many.

More than thirty years ago, long before the discoveries in the Judean desert, the distinguished
Catholic exegete, Father J. M. Lagrange, wrote,
"The more scholarship is brought to bear on the
study of this religious movement [primitive Chris-
tianity], the more we become aware of its Jewish
point of departure, which in no way vitiates its
divine originality." The revelation contained in
the Dead Sea Scrolls is the dazzling corroboration of a truth which ought to be universally recognized. The revelation not only confirms that
truth, but elucidates it and adds enormously to its
substance: it shows that the Jewish roots of Christianity, which go far deeper than had been sup-
posed, are anchored in the fertile soil of what
might be called "marginal" Judaism, lying on the
borderline of official Judaism—an austere and
ascetic Judaism, glowing with a pure and fervent
faith—the faith not, as had sometimes been maintained, of the Pharisees and Rabbi Hillel, but of
the Essenes and of the Teacher of Righteousness,
the Jewish priest who was their leader.

From all of this we are forced to conclude that

pre-Christian Judaism, contrary to the summary
and traditional beliefs set forth at the beginning
of this account, far from being paralyzed, was
imbued and animated by tremendous currents of
intense piety and of mystical spirituality. This
Judaism, which was represented on the one hand
by masters like Hillel and the sages of the Pirke
Avot, on the other by the Teacher of Righteousness, was, though divided, by no means a decadent
religion.

In conclusion, let us admit that before such
overwhelming evidence, tradition—at least in the
higher levels of education in France—has given
way. Is this true in other countries as well? Would
the German theologian Karl Adam, who served as
a member of one of the preparatory commissions
for Vatican II, maintain today what he wrote
twenty years ago, and what was even then in de-
fiance of historical truth? When error has been
broadcast in this manner,[24] it would seem that it
ought to be publicly acknowledged and corrected.

Accordingly, in the hope of a reform in Christian instruction, as long ago as 1947, following a
conference of Christians and Jews in Paris, I drew
up an eighteen-point program, of which Point Four
was as follows:

"To teach, drawing on the most reliable historical research, that Christianity arose not from a
decadent but from a living Judaism, as is proved

by the wealth of Jewish literature, by the indomitable resistance of Judaism to paganism, by the spirituality of the religion practiced in the synagogues, by the spread of proselytism, by the incorporation of new beliefs, and by the multiplicity of sects. To avoid drawing a mere caricature of Pharisaism.''

That same year the Eighteen Points were submitted to the International Congress of Christians and Jews at Seelisberg. A Christian subcommittee, under the chairmanship of Father Calliste Lopinot of Rome, worked out a ten-point program, Point Five of which read, ''To avoid disparaging biblical or post-biblical Judaism for the purpose of exalting Christianity.'' Obviously, this was an oversimplification. Father Démann, who had participated actively in the formulation of the Seelisberg Ten Points, published in 1952 (with the approval of Msgr. de Provenchères, Archbishop of Aix, who was then president of the Episcopal Committee for the Catechism) a brochure, *Les Juifs dans la catéchèse chrétienne,* in which those Ten Points were restated in a slightly different form. Point Three, an expanded version of the original Point Five, read as follows:

To give a true picture of Judaism at the time of Christ, with its atmosphere of crisis and anticipation, taking note of deviations but also of the wealth of its religious life, without oversimplifying to the point of presenting it as utterly decadent. To avoid the same distortion in speaking of later or contemporary Judaism. Any attempt to exalt Christ or Christianity by way of a systematic disparagement of Judaism would be as unworthy as it would be inaccurate. For example, we will avoid comparing the Old Testament with the New as a Law of fear as opposed to a Law of love. At the heart of the religion of Israel there is a boundless confidence in a God of infinite mercy, and its first commandment is to love God with all one's heart. If Christ brings the fullness of this revelation, he likewise insists just as much as the Old Testament did on divine commands and eternal punishments. As for the formalism with which Israel has already been reproached so often by her own prophets, is this not a temptation which threatens the practice of any religion? [25]

Let us give all due respect to these efforts at reform, these signs of respect for the truth. God grant that these aims may be incorporated into the everyday practice of Christian teaching, throughout the Christian world. There is reason to fear that this ideal is still far from realization.

NOTES

1   See Marcel Simon, *Verus Israël,* pp. 255–259, and Jules Isaac, *Genèse de l'antisémitisme,* pp. 161–166.
2   Karl Adam, *The Son of God* (a translation from the German of *Jesus Christus,* London, 1935), p. 183.
3   Killed in July, 1955, when an Israeli Constellation carrying fifty-eight passengers to Israel was attacked without provocation by a Bulgarian aircraft.

4 Cahiers Sioniens, 68, rue Notre-Dame-des-Champs, Paris 6.

5 The sources of these quotations are given by Father Démann in *La catéchèse chrétienne et le peuple de la Bible.*

6 Jules Isaac, *Jésus et Israël,* pp. 74–93 (propositions VII and VIII).

7 The First and Second Books of the Maccabees are included in the canon of the Catholic Bible, but not of the Protestant.

8 Adolphe Lods, *La religion d'Israël* (Paris, 1939), p. 224.

9 *The Apocrypha and Pseudepigrapha of the Old Testament in English,* edited by R. H. Charles (Oxford, 1913), Vol. II.

10 André Dupont-Sommer, *The Essene Writings from Qumran* (Oxford, 1961), p. 263.

11 *Ibid.,* p. 131 (Damascus Document, A: VI: 10–11).

12 *Ibid.,* p. 361.

13 *Ibid.,* pp. 361, 364, 365.

14 *Ibid.,* pp. 76–77.

15 *Ibid.,* pp. 98, 99, 101, 103.

16 *Ibid.,* p. 102.

17 *Ibid.,* pp. 78, 81.

18 *Ibid.,* p. 82.

19 *Ibid.,* p. 92.

20 Jean Daniélou, *The Dead Sea Scrolls and Primitive Christianity* (Baltimore, 1958), p. 35.

21 *Ibid.,* pp. 102, 108.

22 Dupont-Sommer, *op. cit.,* p. 272.

23 Daniélou, *op. cit.,* pp. 125–126.

24 See p. 77.

25 For a complete text of the Eighteen Points, see the author's *Has Anti-Semitism Roots in Christianity?,* published by the National Conference of Christians and Jews (1961).

III

THE CRIME OF DEICIDE

1

*No idea has been more destructive
and has had more deadly effect on the
scattered Jewish minorities living in
Christian countries than the pernicious view of them as the "deicide
people."*

In a recent study, a learned Jesuit Father, review-
ing the various solutions that have been offered to
the problem of responsibility for the Crucifixion,
the first of which was "full responsibility to the
Jews," remarked, "This opinion has not been accepted."

Not accepted, I agree, among the best modern
biblical scholars; but what an overwhelming ac-

ceptance it has had throughout the Christian world, echoing down the centuries even to our own time, with its allegedly objective historiography! I merely report here a historical truth which history itself reveals, at least to those of us who do not choose to avert our eyes, as a tragic, bloodstained reality.[1]

In *Jésus et Israël* I devoted over two hundred pages to this dreadful accusation, the "crime of deicide"; and if I were to rewrite the book today, some fifteen years later, my presentation would be even fuller, tighter, more conclusive. However, within the limits of the present study I shall confine myself to the essential points.

First of all there is the violence, the persistence of an accusation born, like those we have already examined, in the unfortunate climate of Judeo-Christian polemics which became increasingly prevalent between the first and the fourth centuries—a climate that encouraged the worst kind of slander. From this background emerged the recurring theme of murder—of Israel as Cain, as Judas, as a murderous people, a "deicide" people —an epithet at once indelible and absurd, singled out to be an abomination to the Christian world.

By one flourish of the magic wand of theology, old Israel is transformed from a crucified into a crucifying people. All the insults, all the final torments—the flagellation, the nailing of Jesus to the

cross—become the work of the Jews alone. Gone
is the Roman Pontius Pilate, the all-powerful
Procurator of Judea; gone are the Roman soldiers, the executioners; gone is all historical
reality.

In the apocryphal Epistle of Barnabas, written
as early as the end of the first century, we read:
"[The Jews] shall say, 'Is not this He, Whom
once we crucified and set at nought and spat upon.
. . .' "——"For . . . you crucified Him the only
spotless and righteous man," says Justin Martyr
in his second-century *Dialogue with Trypho.* In
the same period, one of the earliest apocryphal
gospels, the so-called Gospel of Peter, assigns the
Jews sole responsibility for the Crucifixion. Thus
nurtured, by the fourth century the theme of deicide has spread throughout the Christian Empire:
"Since their deicide, the Jews have been blinded,
can no longer lead anyone at all," says Eusebius.
"Murderers of the Lord, assassins of the prophets," adds Saint Gregory of Nyssa. "God has forsaken the Jews. They have denied the Father, crucified the Son. . . . Henceforth their Synagogue is
the house of demons and idolatry," continues Saint
John Chrysostom. "In your fathers you have
killed Christ," says Saint Augustine to the Jews.
And to the Christian catechumens he says: "The
Jews, they seize him. . . . The Jews, they bind
him, they crown him with thorns, they spit upon
him, they flagellate him, they heap insults upon

him, they hang him from the wood [of the Cross],
they pierce his flesh with their spears.''

In the preaching and teaching of the Church
Fathers there are, of course, other voices whose
tone and message are more Christian. But it is the
theme of accusation—an accusation of the most
shameful kind—which takes root in impressionable
minds, is incorporated into the liturgy, perpetuated
century after century down to the present, and
takes a striking form in the mystery plays that
flourished from the fourteenth to the sixteenth
centuries.

And if we skip from the fourteenth to the nine-
teenth and twentieth centuries we find the same
theme—the murderous Jews, the Jews as ''dei-
cides'':

''The spectacle of an entire people placed under a
curse for having crucified the Son of God gives
Christians food for thought. . . . This immense
atonement for an infinite crime must continue until the end of the world'': thus Dom Guéranger in
L'Année liturgique. Written in 1841, this is a work
that has influenced many Catholics, that has been
reprinted countless times, and is still so highly
regarded that a century after its original publication the monks of Solesmes brought out a new edition (1948–1952). I do not know whether the latter
has been expurgated of all its anti-Jewish senti-
ments, which were extraordinarily violent. ''The
vengeance of God will fall without mercy on this

deicide people'': thus Father Ferdinand Prat, in
Jésus-Christ. ''The murderous people eternally
nailed to the crossroads where the destinies of
mankind meet and intersect'': thus Father Fessard, in *Pax nostra*. ''The unrivaled shame'' of
the Jewish people who ''slaughtered the Word
made flesh. . . . They had waited more than two
thousand years for the opportunity to crucify the
Word of God'': thus Léon Bloy, in *Le Salut par
les Juifs*. Jean Guitton, in his *Abbé Pouget,* has
his master say, ''The only son put to death by the
vinegrowers represents Christ put to death by the
Jews.'' Giovanni Papini says in *Témoins de la Passion,* ''The Jews and the Jews alone conceived and
desired the deicide.'' Pope Pius XI, in the 1937
Encyclical, *Mit brennender Sorge,* speaks of
''Christ, who received his human nature from a
people which was to crucify him.''

And in the third volume of the *History of the Law
and Institutions of the Western Church,* edited by
Gabriel Le Bras, published in 1958, Jean Gaude-
met explains Christian antagonism as ''hostility
toward the people who put Christ to death.''

These Catholic voices are echoed by those of
Protestants.

''We can see Cain as the prototype of the Jews
who killed our Lord: they carry the mark on their
foreheads,'' says J. N. Darby in his *Introduction
to the Holy Bible*. ''An inner necessity will drive
the Jewish people to nail Jesus to the cross, be-

cause he destroys their pretensions,'' says Gunther Dehn in *The Son of God.* ''[Jesus Christ] called himself King of the Jews. The Jews refused to recognize their king; they mocked him, condemned him to death, crucified him,'' says the Reverend Jean Bosc in *Réforme,* November 23, 1946. ''The Jews stoned the prophets and crucified the Son,'' reads a Declaration by the Reformed Evangelical Church of Basel (and though it proceeds in a less objectionable vein, the accusation of ''deicide'' is not redressed). In *Black Boy,* by the late American Negro author Richard Wright, we read, ''All of us black people who lived in the neighborhood hated Jews, not because they exploited us, but because we had been taught at home and in Sunday school that Jews were 'Christ killers.' '' •

• Because of the inevitable emphasis of French examples in Professor Isaac's text, it is appropriate here to give a few quotations from materials found in analyzing Protestant and Catholic religious education materials in the United States:

When Jesus was in the Temple for the last time, a few days before His Passion, He asked the Jews, "What think ye of Christ?" Their answer was a great disappointment to Him. But on Good Friday they showed what they thought of Him. Their hearts were so filled with hatred toward Him that they shouted themselves hoarse, crying, "Crucify Him!" (Missouri Synod)

Severely bruised and with blood streaming from His body, Jesus was presented to the Jews by Pilate with the pitying appeal, "Behold the man" (in Latin, *Ecce Homo*). . . . The hardhearted, unbelieving Jews could not even thus be moved to pity. (Missouri Synod)

The investigation conducted by Father Démann has shown that around 1950 the vast majority of Catholic schoolbooks in the French language taught the theme of the "deicide people" or even of the "deicide race." [2]

"The destruction of Jerusalem by the Romans [in the year 70] and the final dispersion of the Jews throughout the Empire soon consummated the abrogation of the Law and the punishment of the unbelieving and deicide people."——"This people who live everywhere and rule nowhere, who possess the riches of the world but have no

(Both the examples on the previous page are quoted in Bernhard E. Olson's study. See pages 5, 12, 13.)

The vast majority of the Jewish people . . . condemn Him to death as a blasphemer, and deliver Him up to the Romans to be crucified. (John Laux, *Church History*. New York: Benziger Bros., 1945, p. 7.)

The chief priests took up a cry that put a curse on themselves and on Jews for all time: "His blood be on us and on our children!" (*Living with Christ: High School Religion Course I*, third edition; Winona, Minn.: St. Mary's College Press, 1957, p. 247.)

The curse of Christ and the subsequent decay of the (fig) tree symbolized the condemnation and destruction of the Jewish people for their empty lives. (John C. Dougherty, *Outlines of Bible Study*. Milwaukee, Wis.: The Bruce Publishing Co., 1947, p. 101.)

The Jews as a nation refused to accept Christ, and since His time they have been wanderers on the earth without a temple or a sacrifice and without the Messias. (Francis B. Cassilly, *Religion: Doctrine and Practice*. Chicago: Loyola University Press, 1934, pp. 399–400.)

—EDITOR'S NOTE

home of their own, are born, live and die despised,
ill-treated, and accursed, as if even today there
were written on their foreheads in bloody char-
acters the reason for their disgrace: 'Deicide!' "
To explain the collective guilt of the Jews, eternally weighing them down: "They remain, in spite
of themselves, perpetual witnesses to the fulfillment of the prophecies, and carry everywhere the
visible marks of the curse that weighs down the
deicide people."

We have every reason to assume that the situation is the same in other Catholic countries—Italy,
Spain, Germany, Poland, and the rest. Is it so
astonishing, then, that there should emerge out of
German Catholicism the cruelest, most relentless
advocates of Nazi racism—a Himmler, an Eich-
mann, a Hess? They have only taken and carried
to its logical conclusion a tradition which since the
Middle Ages has been well established throughout
the Christian world—a tradition of hatred and
contempt, of degradation and servitude, of disgrace and violence, on the official as well as the
popular level.

It should be said in defense of the Roman Catholic Church that at least it has never gone as far
as "genocide," that it has always recognized the
right of the Jews to exist as "living testimony,"
and that on occasion it has endeavored to curb the
hatred of the people—after its own teachings had
helped to unleash it.

But it is to our own time, thanks to German racism, that we must award the distinction of outdoing all atrocities, ancient and modern—the autos-da-fé, the medieval massacres, the nineteenth-century Russian pogroms—and of asserting its remarkable superiority over them all with the gas chamber and the crematory oven.

But the scapegoat is with us still; the flow of blood—Jewish blood—is still unstanched. And we are justified in seeing this as the result, not of "deicide," but rather of the Christian accusation of "deicide," repeated over and over again by thousands of voices for almost two thousand years—an accusation which can be readily proved to be evil and unfounded.

2

Christian doctrine here requires that we make careful distinction between the theological and the historical plane. The accusation of "deicide" issues from dangerous confusion of the two.

To begin with, why not appeal to everyday common sense? Common sense tells us that the accusation of "deicide" hurled at the Jewish people is in itself ridiculous and unintelligible. It was in the bosom of the Jewish people that faith in One Omnipotent and Eternal God took form. Such a belief, becoming the unshakable foundation of the religious life of Israel, excluded any possibility of "deicide," or even of understanding the meaning of the word, at any rate for the Jews.

In the Gospel, Jesus subscribes fully to the fundamental article of the Jewish faith. To the scribe who asks him, "Which commandment is the first of all?" he answers, "The first is, Hear, O Israel: The Lord our God, the Lord is one" (Mark 12:28–29). To the man who asks him, "Good Teacher, what must I do to inherit eternal life?" Jesus replies, "Why do you call me good? No one is good but God alone" (Mark 10:17–18; Luke 18:18–9).

To proceed further: The Christian faith, born of the Jewish faith, is based on the mystery of the Incarnation, a mystery which is the object of infinite respect to all religious people, even if they do not embrace it themselves. The Christian Incarnation means that God was incarnate in the human person of the Jew, Jesus of Nazareth, first a simple carpenter, who later preached his gospel, chiefly in Galilee, under the reign of the Emperor Tiberius, around the year 28 of the first century, and who finally, after a year or two of evangelization, was taken prisoner and crucified on the hill of Calvary at Jerusalem. The crucifixion of Jesus is what Christians mean by the term "deicide."

For the charge of "deicide" that has been brought against the Jewish people to have any foundation, certain conditions would have had to be fulfilled. Of these the most important are the following: "Deicide" presupposes on the one hand that Jesus revealed himself to the Jewish people not only as the King-Messiah, the Son of David who had been so feverishly awaited, but also as God Incarnate, the only Son of God, in the fullness of his divine nature. On the other hand it presupposes that the major responsibility for the Crucifixion fell on the Jewish people; and to this we must add that the term "Jewish people" must apply not merely to some minority localized in Palestine, at Jerusalem, but to the Jewish people as a whole, the majority of whom were scattered throughout the pagan world.

We need only name these three necessary conditions, to see that they have not been and never could be met. Jesus had time to make himself known only to a very small minority of Galilean and Judean Jews; the Diaspora was totally ignorant of him. Thus the majority of the Jewish people could have had no share of responsibility in the tragic act of the Crucifixion. Then what qualified biblical scholar would dare state in perfect

honesty that Jesus presented himself openly to the
Jewish people as the "only Son of God" in the fullness of his divine nature? To do so would be to
ignore the most reliable passages in the Gospels.[3]

Let us open the New Testament to the Acts of
the Apostles, and listen to Peter preaching at
Jerusalem: "Men of Israel, hear these words:
Jesus of Nazareth, a man attested to you by God
. . . this Jesus, delivered up according to defi-
nite plan and foreknowledge of God, you crucified and killed by the hands of lawless men
[Romans —J.I.]. . . . This Jesus God raised up,
and of that we all are witnesses. . . . Let all the
house of Israel therefore know assuredly that God
has made him both Lord and Christ, this Jesus
whom you crucified."[4] Again Peter says, "And
now, brethren, I know that you acted in ignorance,
as did also your rulers." (Acts 2:22–24, 32, 36;
3:17) It follows from these passages that the
apostle Peter accused the Jews of Jerusalem not
of "deicide" but of homicide, and homicide
through ignorance. Moreover, they were overcome
with remorse and were baptized *en masse*—three
thousand in Acts 2:41, five thousand in Acts 4:4.
We must read the Book of Acts for a picture of
these early Christian communities, entirely com-
posed of Jews and burning with a fervent faith in
Jesus, become "Lord and Christ" after his death
as a human being. But Catholics rarely read Holy
Scripture; how many of them know that the first

Christians were all Jews, and that primitive Christianity was Judeo-Christianity?

To proceed still further: Christian doctrine teaches both that Jesus was wholly man during his human lifetime and is wholly God. This dual nature, human and divine, has a momentous implication which provides us with the key to the problem we are discussing, the problem of responsibility for the Crucifixion.

Jesus emerges from history during his human lifetime as man and fully man. Assuming that the relevant texts exist, history alone can illuminate for us the respective roles of the Jews and the Romans in Jesus' conviction and his crucifixion on Calvary. In this purely historical inquiry we must work without any preconceptions.

On the Christian level—Jesus as Son of God and possessing the fullness of the divine nature—it is theology that illuminates Jesus and gives full meaning to the Crucifixion. The simplest and clearest statement of that meaning is to be found in Point Seven of the Seelisberg program: "The Cross which saves us all reveals that it was for the sins of all of us that Christ died."

This theological concept, too often ignored by the majority of Christians, is nevertheless perfectly sound Christian doctrine. Although present in embryo in the Epistles of Saint Paul, it only gradually came to assert itself. Apparently it was

first explicitly stated by Pope Gregory the Great
(590–604)—side by side, however, with all the
traditional assertions of Christian anti-Semitism.[5]
Medieval Christianity took very little notice of the
point. Not until we reach the sixteenth century
and the historic Council of Trent (1545–1563) is
the fully expounded doctrine incorporated into the
catechism drawn up at the request of the Council; and only from then on does it represent the
official doctrine of the Church. It reads in part:
"The purpose of the Passion and Death of the
Son of God our Saviour was to redeem and efface
the sins of all time. . . . The sinners themselves
were the authors, the instruments, as it were, of
all the sorrows he endures. . . . We must therefore
hold guilty of this terrible offense all those who
persist in sin. . . . Whenever we deny him again
by our deeds, we are in some sense raising our
deicide hands against him."

From the point of view of theology, then, Jewish
responsibility is subordinated to the collective responsibility of sinful humanity. Or if you prefer a
symbolic interpretation, the Jewish people are but
an image of humanity as a whole.

In either event, who is the real culprit, the real
"deicide"? The human race, the whole of sinful
mankind.

When the Catholic author Charles Péguy writes,
"It was not the Jews who crucified Jesus Christ,
but all our sins; and the Jews, who were only the

instrument, partake with the others at the fount of
salvation,'' he is simply expressing the doctrine
of the Church on the plane of theology. But the
statement that the Jews were the ''instrument''
of the Passion, of the Crucifixion, is historical, and
it is now the task of historical inquiry to show
whether it has any foundation.

3

*The Crucifixion is an historical event,
and cannot be studied without refer-
ence to its historical setting.*

The Crucifixion is located chronologically
around the year 29 or 30, under the reign of the
Roman emperor Tiberius, adopted son of and suc-
cessor to Augustus. What was the situation in
Jewish Palestine at that time?

The last thirty years had seen profound changes.
The chief of these was the growing oppressiveness
of Roman domination, which had become more
and more intolerable to the Jewish population in
Galilee, as well as in Judea.

The Jews of Palestine cherished the thrilling
memory of the victorious wars of liberation they
had waged, under the leadership of the Maccabees,

against the powerful Greek armies of the Seleucids. These wars had resulted, at the end of the
second century B.C., in the restoration of a Jewish
kingdom in Palestine. But after the Greek armies
came the Roman legions. The Jewish kings had
tried to remain friendly with the Roman authorities. In this, Herod the Great had been especially
successful: a half-Jew hated for his cruelty, he
had reigned over a prosperous state for more than
thirty years (37–4 B.C.) and had endowed Jerusalem
with a magnificent building for that unique sanctuary, the Temple.

But that epoch was over, and Rome was tighten-
ing its hold over all of the Near East. Judea and
Samaria, the leading provinces of Herod's old
kingdom, had passed into the control of a Roman
procurator; Herod's two sons had been left with
only the remaining territories, which they ruled as
tetrarchs. Galilee, where Jesus lived, was under
the rule of the tetrarch Herod Antipas.

Harsh though it was, the Roman protectorate
permitted a certain degree of local autonomy. To
collect as much money as possible from the subject populations, to maintain peace and order, to
keep tight curb on all rebellion—these were the
most important tasks of the Roman government.
In all other respects the Jews were free to live their
lives according to their lights, following their own
customs. In Judea, under the Roman Procurator,
the ruling power was vested in a Great Council,

or Sanhedrin, presided over by the high priest in office and made up of high priests, men of wealth, and a few Pharisee teachers. Most of the political and legal power was in the hands of the high priests; they were chosen from among three or four families, always the same ones, and formed a tyrannical, narrowly conservative oligarchy, closely allied with the Roman government, which appointed or dismissed them at will. Their subordination was such that the high priest in office did not even have charge of the sacerdotal furnishings, which were kept under lock and key by the Roman guard at Fort Antonia in Jerusalem.

Servile in its relations with the Roman overlords, tyrannical in its relations with the Jewish people, this oligarchy kept a certain degree of control because of its sacerdotal authority, and also because of the Temple, the unique sanctuary of Judaism, as well as the large staff of subordinates at its disposal. Ostensibly, the High Priest at Jerusalem was the official leader of the Jewish world, but his moral and spiritual authority was hardly commensurate with his high rank.

And how could it have been otherwise? The high priests and the wealthy and prominent in Jerusalem were the only ones who agreed to the humiliating collaboration with Rome. Elsewhere the prevailing sentiment among Palestinian Jews was a hatred for the pagan oppressor and a burning desire for freedom—a desire which fre-

quently took a messianic form. Monotheism, the
expectation of the King-Messiah, and the love of
independence were inseparably interwoven with
this anti-Roman feeling, which was continually
ready to flare up in fierce rebellions.

These feelings are echoed in several passages in
the Gospels. One is the Benedictus, as spoken by
the priest Zechariah (Luke 1: 68 ff.): "Blessed be
the Lord God of Israel, for he has visited and re-
deemed his people, and has raised up a horn of
salvation for us in the house of his servant David,
. . . that we should be saved from our enemies,
and from the hand of all that hate us." After the
Crucifixion, what do the disciples say on the road
to Emmaus? They remember Jesus of Nazareth as
"a prophet mighty in deed and word before God
and all the people, and . . . had hoped that he was
the one to redeem Israel" [the implication is, from
Roman oppression] (Luke 24: 19, 21).

The cruelty with which all revolts were sup-
pressed added to the fury of the people. In the
course of the confusion following the death of
Herod, Varus, governor of Syria, who was sent to
intervene in Judea, ordered the crucifixion of two
thousand Jews. Two thousand men were subjected
to the most ignominious form of punishment de-
vised by the Romans, death on the cross, a mon-
strous, unforgettable vision of hell. And how many
like it were to follow! Galilee, too, was a hotbed
of rebellion: it was the birthplace of Jewish ter-
rorism, the faction of the zealots, the sicarii,

who were renewing their attacks and preparing
for a holy war. Could Jesus, living in Galilee, possibly have been unaware of them? In fact, there
were zealots among his first disciples.[6] Keeping
an eye on zealotry, and suppressing it, were among
the chief worries of the Roman government; for
this reason, any disturbance was suspect.

Between these two extreme positions—of the
high priests who were collaborators and puppets of
Rome and the zealots eager for a holy war—there
were, of course, intermediate attitudes. The members of the two main religious sects, the Pharisees
and the Essenes, were anti-Roman at heart, but
refusing to resort to rebellion and force, they left
to God and the Messiah the task of liberating the
Jewish people.

From this brief but precise résumé, at least two
conclusions may be drawn. The first is that at the
time of Jesus, Jewish Palestine, and especially
Galilee, was full of unrest, seething with anti-
Roman feeling. If Jesus had presented himself to
the people not as God incarnate or even as his only
Son, but as the liberating King-Messiah, the Son
of David, what a formidable revolution he would
have launched!—one that would immediately have
provoked the most brutal reaction on the part of
the Roman authorities.

This may explain the messianic silence which
Jesus imposed on his disciples during the conversation on the road to Caesarea: "Then he

strictly charged the disciples that they should tell
no man that he was the Christ" (Matthew 16:20;
Luke 9:21). And at bottom the same is true, all
appearances to the contrary, of the Fourth Gospel, for after the miracle of the loaves, "perceiving
then that they were about to come and take him
by force, to make him king [King-Messiah—J.I.],
Jesus withdrew again to the hills by himself"
(John 6:15).

Our second conclusion may be briefly sum-
marized: At the time of Christ in Palestine, who
did the crucifying? The Romans. Who was crucified? The Jews.

It remains to be seen how and why the victims
came to be transformed into the executioners—a
phenomenon which would appear at first glance
to be utterly inexplicable.

4

*The Gospels, our only source of infor-
mation on the Crucifixion, are works
of religious teaching and persuasion,
and are not concerned with
historical accuracy.*

What do we know about the trial of Jesus, the
trial that resulted in his death sentence and his

crucifixion? Historians have neither a written transcript, as they do of the trial of Joan of Arc, nor reliable contemporary testimony. They have nothing to go on but the account given in the Gospels.

In *Jésus et Israël* [7] I have mentioned my respect for "those venerable texts by which was revealed to the world a message which will always sustain the human heart." On the other hand, as I wrote then, "a respect for history, for its demands of integrity," obliges us to admit that "the documentary value of the Gospels, especially concerning such an event as the Passion, is extremely difficult to determine."

The fact is recognized today by all biblical scholars, including Catholic ones, that the primary intention of the Gospel writers was to serve their faith in Jesus Christ. The Gospels are works of religious instruction and persuasion whose purpose is to "demonstrate" the truths of the religion. It follows, not that the texts are devoid of historical value, but that we must read them critically if we are to disentangle some scraps of historical truth from this instruction. This is all the more true, since on several important points the four Gospels disagree.

Let us note here some views expressed by qualified Catholic writers. Father Joseph Bonsirven writes: "The Evangelists did not intend to write an accurate history as we understand it today, but

to create a vehicle of demonstration." Likewise
H. I. Marrou: "The Gospel writer did not set out
to provide a record of history as it was being made,
but something altogether different; his intention
was to transmit to his readers, from the standpoint
of the teaching of the Church, the knowledge of
Christ necessary for salvation." Or Father X.
Léon-Dufour: "The Evangelists do not seem to
have wanted to be historians in our sense of the
word. . . . The Gospels must be read as examples
of their literary genre, as sacred history written
to stimulate and reinforce faith." Certain Protestant scholars go even further; for them the Gospels
are in no sense historical documents, but are "religious documents showing what Jesus meant in
terms of the faith and piety of the milieu in which
they were written"; thus, the life and Passion of
Jesus are known to us only "through images be-
longing to the culture which gave birth to the
culture which gave birth to the Gospels."

It is not enough to realize that the Evangelists'
accounts are essentially religious instruction rather
than history. One must be alert to the fact that
these accounts, at the period when they were given
their definitive form, were themselves inseparable
from a particular historical milieu, which they in-
evitably reflect. Honesty demands that textual crit-
icism give careful consideration to this fact.
    When were the four canonical Gospels set down?

We do not know with certainty; qualified scholars agree that it was during the last third of the first century, allowing for later modifications. The oldest manuscripts of the Gospels go back only as far as the fourth century.

Let us look at the situation of the youthful Church, the new Christian religion, in the last third of the first century. How many changes it had seen since the time of its birth! First of all, its ultimate break with the Synagogue: primitive Christianity, or Judeo-Christianity, was no more than an isolated sect, and was soon denounced as heretical. After the Church's rejection of the Torah, the recruitment of the Jews was coming to a halt; the Christian apostolate, following the example of Saint Paul, had turned to the pagan Gentiles. After the bloody and relentless Judean war (66–70), which aroused a wave of anti-Jewish feeling in Rome, the Christians decided to sever their connection with the Jews, their estranged brothers, and to conciliate public opinion and the Roman authorities. Hence a characteristic of the Evangelists' accounts of the Passion is their common tendency to reduce Roman responsibility to the minimum and to exaggerate Jewish responsibility to the maximum.

This is so obvious that it has come to be acknowledged, even by Catholic exegetes. As early as 1928 Father Léonce de Grandmaison was writing: "It is permissible to think that in the very wording of the Synoptic Gospels the notion, from then on an accepted one, of the mass obduracy of the Jewish people made its first appearance.'' In 1960 Father Léon-Dufour put it more frankly: ''In the main, the Jews were more and more accused, the Romans more and more excused . . . probably because the Christian apostolate was turning toward the pagans.'' The impartial historian Marcel Simon is even more explicit: ''The authors [of the Gospels], anxious to humor Rome, visibly took pains to present the Passion in such a way that the Roman government, represented by Pilate, comes out of the affair practically spotless, while the Jews are weighed down with a guilt which they openly admit.''

What conclusions may be drawn from this preliminary examination? That the historian has a right and a duty, an absolute duty, to see the Gospel accounts of the Passion as testimony weighted against the Jews. Now, let us ask ourselves honestly whether, if we had nothing to go on but Jewish traditions, written in the spirit of an apology, we would accept *them* without reservation? Of course we would not: the converse is true.

In support of these generalizations it seems necessary to give two concise, conclusive examples —one provided by a careful analysis of the Gospel texts, the other by a comparison of certain historical facts with those texts.

Our first example is taken from a remarkable recent work by a learned biblical scholar, Paul Winter's *On the Trial of Jesus*.[8] The critical study he has made of the accounts of the Passion sheds light on a fact that is surprising, even startling: the name of the high priest in office is unknown, or incorrectly known, to the Evangelists. What? The high priest, to whom they assign the leading role and the gravest responsibilities, they do not even know his name? Their uncertainty is especially strange in that the high priest then in office —who according to Josephus was Caiphas—held his position for eighteen years (18–36), a tenure that is quite extraordinary and implies great submissiveness toward the Roman Procurator (who from the year 26 up until 36 was Pontius Pilate: of this name not one of the Evangelists has any doubt).

No name is given to the high priest in the Gospel of Mark, acknowledged to be the oldest of the four. No name is given to the high priest in the account by Luke of the Passion. Later, as anti-Jewish prejudice grew in Christian circles, it became necessary to fill an awkward gap, and to name the high priest involved; this, each of the writers did in his own way. Only Matthew, better informed on Jewish affairs than the others, belatedly gave the name of Caiphas. If we examine closely the Gospels according to Luke and John, we find the name inaccurately given as Annas. For the sake of con-

sistency the name of Caiphas was later added to
that of Annas in Luke 3:2 and in Acts 4:6. In the
Gospel of John, the name Caiphas has been in-
terpolated as being that of the son-in-law of Annas, but it is obvious that in John 18:19–33 Annas
is the officiating high priest who interrogates
Jesus; everything relating to Caiphas has been
rather ineptly added.

On the basis of this ignorance and uncertainty,
Paul Winter is then perfectly justified in deduc-
ing that "the hierarch's [high priest's] part in the
proceedings against Jesus was far from being as
prominent as the Evangelists suggest." [9] This
simple observation also indicates the extent to
which the Gospel tradition in regard to the Passion was, at the outset, divorced from certain
fundamental realities.

But other realities were inescapable. A Roman punishment, the Cross erected on Calvary
pointed the finger of guilt not toward Caiphas but
toward Pilate. Nothing could have been more in-
convenient or troublesome for the Christian apostolate, anxious at all costs to placate the Roman
government. How were they to cope with the difficulty? Each of the Evangelists did the best he
could, in his own fashion—which brings us to our
second example, the vital confrontation between
the data of history and those of the Evangelists.

For we have historical information concerning
the matter. As we have seen, we have information

concerning the Jewish people who were then so passionately anti-Roman, so ripe for revolt. We have information on the procurators, and especially on Pontius Pilate, showing him for what he really was—a bloodthirsty tyrant.[10] As a witness against him we have, first of all, his contemporary (and therefore the contemporary of Jesus), the distinguished Jewish philosopher Philo of Alexandria, who mentions "the crimes [of Pilate], his rages, his greed, his injustices, his abuses, the citizens he had put to death without trial, his intolerable cruelty." In the next generation the Jewish historian Flavius Josephus tells of three incidents in the governorship of Pilate, two of which resulted in massacres. Another witness is Luke the Evangelist himself, who mentions (13:1) a massacre of Galileans ordered by Pilate.

Modern Catholic exegesis is obliged to admit that (as Father Léon-Dufour puts it) "the behavior of Pilate in the Gospel accounts seems to be out of keeping with the data of history." In short, the bloodthirsty tyrant has been transformed in the Gospel accounts of the Passion into an honest man, anxious to find Jesus innocent and to save his life, who yields in spite of himself before the furious pressure of the Jews—not only of the Jewish leaders but of the people themselves, bent on bringing about the crucifixion of Jesus, one of their own people, by the hated Roman.

Here we have the successful metamorphosis of

a crucified into a crucifying people, which may be
in the interest of catechism, but is clearly not in
the interest of historical truth.

5

*In the last analysis, and despite the
difficulty of the task, we must try to
discover whatever remnants of historical truth lurk behind the Christian
instruction contained in the
stories of the Passion.*

How difficult a task this is we have made clear
in pointing out that the Gospel accounts, our only
source of information, are essentially religious instruction and not history. The task is made even
more difficult by the individual biases, the discrepancies, and the contradictions in these four
accounts.

We must admit that history based on foundations
such as these is reduced to mere guesswork, with
no great hope of attaining certainty. To be sure,
historical certainty is much rarer than we think:
history itself is conjectural knowledge.

Still, it is possible to find a clue to guide us

through the turns of the Gospel labyrinth, thanks precisely to this obvious tendency on the part of the Evangelists more and more to blame the Jews and exonerate the Romans. Father Léon-Dufour accordingly concludes that historical validity may be accorded to certain observations in the Fourth Gospel because they go "against the prevailing bias." An excellent point, but why limit it to the Gospel of John? Extend it to the four canonical Gospels, and we have our clue.

In this way, we may glean from the four stories one primary and essential fact: The measures taken against Jesus at Jerusalem were taken without the knowledge of the people, in spite of the people, and through fear of the people. What people? Obviously, the Jewish people: the common people, that mass of good, simple folk to whom Jesus chose to address himself and who listened to him enthralled. Why hold all the Jewish people, "the whole race of Israel," forever responsible, along with their unworthy leaders—with a man like Caiphas, or with the high priesthood as a whole? Why dissociate the Jews from those sympathetic multitudes who crowded around Jesus?

"And the chief priests and the scribes heard it," we read in Mark 11: 18, "and sought a way to destroy him; for they feared him, because all the multitude was astonished at his teaching." Similar observations are found in Mark 12: 12 and 14: 1-2;

again in Matthew 21: 45–46, 26: 3–5; and in Luke
19: 47, 22: 1–6. The opposition between the people
and their leaders is also apparent in John
11: 47–48: "So the chief priests and the Pharisees
gathered the council, and said, 'What are we to
do? For this man performs many signs. If we let
him go on thus, everyone will believe in him, and
the Romans will come and destroy both our holy
place and our nation.' "

But, it will be objected, is this not a contradiction of the passage already quoted, in which the
apostle Peter says to the Jews of Jerusalem,
"This Jesus . . . you crucified and killed by the
hands of lawless men"? (Acts 2: 22–24) The contradiction is, however, more apparent than real:
the Book of Acts agrees, since it is the work of the
same author, with the Gospel of Luke, and thus it
presupposes a complete about-face on the part of
the people, which on the historical level is impossible to accept. As for Peter, who denied Jesus at
the time of his Passion, it would be more accurate
if he had said, "This Jesus . . . *we* crucified and
killed. . . ." For Jesus' disciples, being the best-
informed of his authority, are more to be blamed
for having deserted him.

In the second place, by whom was the fatal decision made? The four Gospel accounts reply that
it was the Jewish leaders; they say nothing about
the Roman officialdom which nevertheless was the
supreme authority. Now, given the circumstances

of time and place—the fact that it was the eve of the
Passover; that at that time the holy city was
swarming with a huge, turbulently emotional
crowd, from which the zealots were certainly not
absent; that the Procurator was there, having
made a special trip from his residence in Caesarea
to see that order was maintained and to quell any
disturbances—it seems obvious that the Roman
government must have played a part in the affair.
Even if its intervention was not immediate and
decisive, there must have been co-operation between the Jewish and Roman authorities.

Again we must differentiate the various Jewish
leaders with more care than the Gospels do—especially the last to be written, the Gospel of John.
He brings the Pharisees into the matter because,
at the time he was writing, the Pharisees had become the bitter enemies of the Christians. But it is
extremely doubtful whether half a century earlier,
such Pharisee leaders as Gamaliel, the true spiritual guides of the Jewish people, would have
taken part in the movement to suppress Jesus.
The position of Gamaliel seems to be well defined
in Acts 5: 35–39: "Men of Israel, take care what
you do with these men. . . . Keep away from these
men and let them alone; for if this plan or this
undertaking is of men, it will fail; but if it is of
God, you will not be able to overthrow them. You
might even be found opposing God!"

As for Pilate, he did not look so closely into the

matter. To him any form of messianism was suspect because it meant unrest on the part of the
people. Now, Jesus' entrance into Jerusalem had
a messianic quality; Jesus was hailed by his followers as "Son of David" (Mark 11: 10; Matthew
21: 9), as "King" (Luke 19: 38), and as "King of
Israel" (John 12: 13). This was more than enough
to call down Roman retribution.

As a proof—and this is our third point—there is
the arrest of Jesus. John is the only one of the
Evangelists who mentions the intervention of the
Roman soldiers, and this is so uncharacteristic of
him that the authenticity of the fact seems thereby
assured. Who is going to believe that these Roman
soldiers and their superior officer were acting on
the orders of Judas or Caiphas? They were acting
on orders from Pilate, who had sent them. Had the
Procurator acted of his own free will or at the request of the High Priest? It is impossible to say.
Along with the Roman soldiers were the Temple
guard (John 18: 3)—further proof of the co-operation we have already mentioned. Christian tradition has it that in this co-operation the initiative,
the leading role, belongs to the Jewish authorities,
and that they therefore have the major responsibility. Initiative is something which is almost impossible to determine. But common sense tells us
that in such cases the greatest responsibility lies
with those who command the greatest power—in
other words, with Pilate. And what happened next
is ample proof that this is so.

What happened to Jesus after he was taken prisoner and bound? While waiting to appear before
Pilate, he was led to the house of the High Priest,
who had undoubtedly been authorized by the Procurator to make a preliminary investigation. Three
of the four Gospels mention one and even two appearances of Jesus before the Sanhedrin; the
Gospel of John again differs from the other three
in making no mention of a Jewish trial: in the
Fourth Gospel there is only one trial, and that is
the Roman trial. Using our clue, we must put our
confidence in John on this fourth point.

For a long time the accepted view was that
Jesus, having first been indicted before the Sanhedrin, had been condemned to death by it for blasphemy, and that the Jewish authorities had handed
him over to Pilate because they had lost the right
to pronounce or execute the death sentence. This
view encountered so much opposition that it was
abandoned by judicious scholars. Father Léon-
Dufour recognizes (just as I did in *Jésus et Israël* [11]), that "we cannot be sure that the Sanhedrin
did not have the power to exercise the *jus gladii*
[the right of execution]"; but also, vis-à-vis the
Roman authorities, that "in certain cases, the Sanhedrin acted as a court of interrogation, a court of
arraignment." Such would have been its function
in the case of Jesus.

Today I would go still further, and subscribe to
the compelling argument of Paul Winter, namely
that the Sanhedrin maintained all of its judiciary

power, particularly in religious affairs, so that if Jesus had been sentenced to die for blasphemy by that body, according to Jewish custom he would have been executed, as his disciple Stephen later was, by stoning.

If we hold fast to the information supplied by the Gospel of John, we find nothing to indicate that the Sanhedrin was consulted. Brought into the house of the High Priest, Jesus appeared before the latter and his assistants, among whom there may have been some members of the Sanhedrin (John 18:19, 28). Did the High Priest not have full authority to prosecute Jesus at the meeting of the Sanhedrin prior to the arrest? (John 11: 47–48)—an authority otherwise strictly limited by the fact of Roman intervention. For—and this is notable—it was not the Jews who handed Jesus over to the Romans, but the Romans who, for a few hours, delivered him to the Jews, in the person of the High Priest.

Thus after the Roman intervention there was— there could only have been—a single trial, and that was the Roman trial. Jesus stands before Pilate: his life and death are in the hands of Pilate, and of Pilate alone. Say what you will, this is the incontestable truth that dominates the story of the Passion.

What is the crime of which Jesus is accused? The sign placed on the Cross, the *titulus*, tells us very clearly: It reads, "King of the Jews" (Mark

15 : 26). It was as a king, or as a pretender to kingship—the kingship of the Messiah—that Jesus was
sentenced and crucified.

Messianic agitation was not considered a crime
by the Jews—far from it, even though it was
feared by the high priests because they were anxious to maintain the established order from which
they were profiting. It was a crime only in the
eyes of the Romans, for whom any messianic agitation was tantamount to the crime of rebellion
against Rome, and was punished as such. To be
sure, Jesus was not a zealot, but Pilate could easily
have mistaken him for one; it was perhaps as a
zealot, but in any case as a rebel, that Jesus was
arrested by the Romans, tried by them, convicted,
and crucified.

Crucifixion was not a Jewish but a Roman penalty, the most ignominious and painful penalty
there was—and how many Jews had suffered
that fate since the Roman occupation! The crucifixion of Jesus and the flagellation and crowning
with thorns that preceded it were the work of
the Roman soldiers alone.

Luke 23 : 27 depicts Jesus making his way pain-
fully up Calvary, followed by "a great multitude
of the people, and of women who bewailed and
lamented him." While Jesus was crucified, "the
people stood by, watching"—from a distance, no
doubt, and in silence (Luke 23 : 35). When Jesus
gave up the ghost, this crowd "returned home

beating their breasts'' (Luke 23:48). Is this the
description of a crowd bent on Jesus' destruction?
No, these are people who are frightened, who are
overcome with grief.

Once again our clue leads us, through the account given by Luke, to the real attitude of the
Jewish people throughout the Passion, the attitude
consistent with the data of history. What, then,
remains of the myth of the deicide people and their
crime of crucifixion? Nothing but the perversity
of habit.

Jesus died the victim of Roman authority, sentenced by Pilate, crucified by Roman soldiers.
Nothing, not even the co-operation of the Jewish
authorities, can extenuate the significance of this
historical fact, whose certainty is beyond question.

Such are the conclusions of an investigation
conducted on a purely historical level—conclusions
which are limited but essential. All the rest is the
product of Christian catechism—whose orientation
we know—which, because of its orientation, was
too often exploited to foster and support the worst
prejudices.

This is half admitted in the seventh point of the
Seelisberg program: ''To avoid presenting the
Passion in such a way that the odium of the execu-
tion of Jesus falls on all the Jews and on the Jews
alone. . . . To remind all parents and educators
of the solemn responsibility they incur in present-

ing . . . the story of the Passion in an oversim-
plified manner. . . . Psychologically speaking, to
persons of limited intelligence . . . the abhorrence
they quite naturally feel toward Jesus' tormentors
easily turns into a generalized hatred of the Jews
of all times, including those of today."

Indeed, there is only one way of preventing this,
and that is to recognize the truth, to state explicitly
that the Jewish people as a whole are in no way
responsible for the Crucifixion. Father Léon-
Dufour, author of the most recent Catholic study
(1960), concedes that "one cannot assign collective
guilt to the people alive at the time of the events"
—with this reservation—"except for such as
allowed themselves to be bribed by those in
power." But need such mercenary rabble, the like
of which are to be found in every time and place,
be brought into it at all? John (19:6) does not
even mention them; he speaks only of "the chief
priests and the officers."

At the end of the present study, the author ex-
pects to be accused of prejudice, dismissed as an
apologist—the eternal story of the mote in our
neighbor's eye and the beam in our own. What
has not been done in the last nineteen hundred
years in an effort to conjure away Pilate! At
which juncture I shall undoubtedly be accused of
trying to conjure away Caiphas. Far be it from
me to undertake such a dismal assignment: The

Jewish high priest at the time of Jesus strikes
me as no more worth defending than Pierre Cau-
chon, the very Catholic Bishop of Beauvais at the
time of Joan of Arc. Caiphas and the Jewish high
priests have their share of responsibility; we have
in no way concealed it, but have contented ourselves with restoring them to the subordinate position which history assigns them. By the same
token Pilate, the Roman magistrate, has also been
restored to the position in Judea that history
assigns him: the pre-eminent one, with the full and
total responsibility his supreme power implies.

Is there anything unpardonable in this? No in-
jury has been done the Christian religion. It is
the mythical and unhappy tradition of the "deicide
people" that does violence to truth, justice, the dig-
nity of Israel—the Israel of old—and even to her
right to live.

For the Christian religion does not require for
her own glorification a corresponding disparagement of ancient Israel, of the people of the Old
Testament, the people of Jesus and the Apostles,
and of the first Christians.

God give her the power to break at last with
these evil habits of mind and heart and tongue,
contracted over a period of nearly two thousand
years as a result of what I have called the teaching
of contempt—itself the child of bitter polemics
now obsolete.

God be thanked, a purifying stream exists in

Christianity and grows stronger every day. This book is fresh evidence, however, that this new attitude is still far from having prevailed. Evil habits persist; they are too old to be uprooted overnight. All the more reason to persevere in our efforts, to strive without ceasing to attain the desired end— the necessary reappraisal of Christian education regarding Israel, a reappraisal which will also be an atonement; a work of truth, but also of justice, and one which I am convinced is of the greatest significance and will have infinitely beneficial consequences for Christianity as well as for Judaism.

NOTES

1   Jules Isaac, "Problèmes de la Passion d'après deux études récentes," *Revue Historique*, July–September, 1961, p. 127.
2   Démann, *La catéchèse chrétienne et le peuple de la Bible,* pp. 122–123, 130, 160, 163, 167–168, 171.
3   See Jules Isaac, *Jésus et Israël*, pp. 215–276 (proposition XIV).
4   But is even this accusation of Peter's valid? See Part 5 (p. 138).
5   See Jules Isaac, *Genèse de l'antisémitisme*, pp. 289–291.
6   The significance of the zealot movement in society and in connection with the death of Jesus is especially well set forth by O. Cullmann in *Dieu et César* (1956).
7   *Jésus et Israël*, p. 425.
8   See the author's analysis of this book in *Revue Historique*, 1961, No. 3, pp. 127–137.
9   Paul Winter, *On the Trial of Jesus* (Berlin, 1961), p. 39.
10   See passages quoted in *Jésus et Israël*, pp. 453–456.
11   *Ibid.*, pp. 409–411.

APPENDIX

Jules Isaac's *Jésus et Israël* was placed before my eyes, as
if by chance, at a time when I was seeking to clarify some
ideas on this problem which is closer to my heart than
any other. A first reading of the twenty-one propositions
which form the backbone of this work is so overwhelming
in its effect that one dare not remain silent while Israel
is raising such a cry of anguish. The author is often right;
it is disgraceful how right he is, and it would be just as
disgraceful for us not to try to answer him; for many of
the charges he brings against us are, I fear, the same ones
by which we will one day be undone before a Judge infinitely more powerful than he. For there is no escaping
the fact that we Christians are almost all responsible in
degrees which vary mysteriously from one soul to the
next, according to our capacity for understanding; and
Jesus' Passion continues to be acted out night and day
in the world. Once having been nailed on the Roman
cross, he has been persecuted through his own race with
inexorable cruelty. We cannot raise our hand against a
Jew without striking with the same blow him who is the
man *par excellence* and, at the same time, the flower of
Israel; and it is Jesus who suffered in the concentration

camps; it is always he, his suffering is never ended. Ah, to be done with all this, and to begin all over again! To meet on the morning of the Resurrection and to clasp Israel to our hearts, weeping, without a word. For after Auschwitz, only tears can have meaning. Christian, wipe the tears and the blood from the face of your Jewish brother, and the countenance of your Christ will shine upon you both.

—Julien Green, *Journal*
in *Revue de Paris*, June, 1949

LIST OF PROPOSITIONS
IN *JÉSUS ET ISRAËL*

Introduction:
A Preliminary Look at the Old Testament

I. The Christian religion is the daughter of the Jewish religion. The New Testament of the Christians is built upon the foundation of the Old Testament of the Jews. If only for this reason, Judaism is deserving of respect.

Part I: *Jesus the Christ,*
a Jew "According to the Flesh"

II. Jesus, the Jesus of the Gospels, only Son and Incarnation of God for the Christians, in his human lifetime was a Jew, a humble Jewish artisan. This is a fact which no Christian has a right to ignore.

III. Insofar as we can know of them through the Gospels, Jesus' family was Jewish: Mary, his mother, was Jewish, and so were all their friends and relatives. To be at once an anti-Semite and a Christian is to try to marry reverence with abuse.

IV. On each New Year's Day the Church commemorates the circumcision of the Infant Jesus. It was not without hesitation and controversy that early Christianity abandoned this rite sanctioned by the Old Testament.

V. The name Jesus Christ is essentially Semitic, even though its form is Greek: *Jesus* is the hellenization of a Jewish name, and *Christ* is the Greek equivalent of the Jewish word *Messiah*.

VI. The New Testament was written in Greek. The Catholic Church quotes it in Latin, a Latin which is the result of translation. But Jesus, like all the Palestinian Jews he was addressing, spoke Aramaic, a Semitic language closely related to Hebrew.

Part II: *The Gospel in the Synagogue*

VII. It is commonly maintained that at the time of the coming of Christ, the Jewish religion had degenerated into a mere legalism without a soul. History does not support this verdict. In spite of Jewish legalism and its excesses, everything at this period attests to the depth and intensity of the religious life of Israel.

VIII. The teaching of Jesus took place in the traditional Jewish setting. According to a very liberal Jewish

custom, "the carpenter's son" was permitted to speak
and teach in the synagogues, and even in the Temple at
Jerusalem.

IX. Jesus was born and lived "under the [Jewish]
Law." Did he intend or announce its abrogation? Many
writers hold that he did, but their statements exaggerate,
distort, or contradict the most important passages in the
Gospels.

X. Nothing would be more futile than to try to separate from Judaism the Gospel that Jesus preached in the
synagogues and in the Temple. The truth is that the Gospel and its entire tradition are deeply rooted in Jewish
tradition.*

Part III: *Jesus and His People*

XI. Christian writers deliberately omit the fact that
at the time of Christ the "Dispersion" of the Jews had
been a *fait accompli* for several centuries. The majority
of the Jewish people no longer lived in Palestine.

XII. Therefore, no one has any right to say that the
Jewish people "as a whole" rejected Jesus. It is entirely
probable that the Jewish people "as a whole" were not
even aware of his existence.

XIII. But, with rare exceptions, wherever Jesus went
the Jewish people took him to their hearts, as the Gospels
testify. Did they, at a given moment, suddenly turn

* Since the publication of the manuscripts discovered in the
cave of Ain Feschka, we should add, "and in the attempts at
renovation and purification which had been manifested for almost two centuries in Palestine."

against him ? This is a notion which has yet to be proved.

XIV. In any case, no one has the right to declare that the Jewish people rejected Christ or the Messiah, that they rejected the Son of God, until it is proved that Jesus revealed himself as such to the Jewish people "as a whole," and was rejected by them as such. But the Gospels give us good reason to doubt that this ever happened.

XV. Christ is said to have pronounced a sentence of condemnation and alienation on the Jewish people. But why, in contradiction of his own gospel of love and forgiveness, should he have condemned his own people, the only people to whom he chose to speak—his own people, among whom he found not only bitter enemies, but fervent disciples and adoring followers? We have every reason to believe that the real object of his condemnation is a certain pharisaism to be found in all times and in all peoples, in every religion and in every church.

Part IV: *The Crime of Deicide*

XVI. For eighteen hundred years it has been generally taught throughout the Christian world that the Jewish people, in full responsibility for the Crucifixion, committed the inexpiable crime of "deicide." No accusation could be more pernicious—and in fact none has caused more innocent blood to be shed.

XVII. Now, in the Gospels, Jesus was careful to name in advance the parties responsible for the Passion: the pontiffs, the dignitaries, and doctors of the Law—a common species no more limited to the Jews than to any other people.

XVIII. Joan of Arc was also sentenced by a tribunal of chief priests and scribes—who were not Jewish—but only after a long trial of which we have the complete and authentic text. This is not true of the trial of Jesus, which was hurried through in a few hours and is known only by hearsay. No official transcript, no contemporary testimony on the event has come down to us.

XIX. To establish the responsibility of the Jewish people in the Roman trial, the Roman death sentence, and the Roman penalty, we must ascribe to certain passages in the Gospels an historical validity which is particularly dubious; we must overlook their discrepancies, their improbabilities, and give them an interpretation which is no less biased and arbitrary for being traditional.

XX. To crown its injustices, a certain so-called Christian element, only too happy to fall in with a secular prejudice which is complicated by ignorance or misunderstanding of the Gospel, has never wearied of using the grievous theme of the Crucifixion against the Jewish people as a whole.

CONCLUSION

XXI. Whatever the sins of Israel may be, she is totally innocent of the crimes of which Christian tradition accuses her : She did not reject Jesus and she did not crucify him. And Jesus did not reject Israel, did not curse her : Just as ''the gifts of God are irrevocable'' (Romans

11 : 29), the evangelical Law of love allows no exception. May Christians come to realize this at last—may they realize and redress their crying injustices. At this moment, when a curse seems to weigh upon the whole human race, it is the urgent duty to which we are called by the memory of Auschwitz.